ROUTLEDGE LIBRARY EDITIONS:
EDUCATION

EDUCATION

EDUCATION
A Search for New Principles

HERBERT PHILLIPSON

Volume 150

Routledge
Taylor & Francis Group
LONDON AND NEW YORK

First published in 1942

This edition first published in 2012
by Routledge
2 Park Square, Milton Park, Abingdon, Oxfordshire OX14 4RN

Simultaneously published in the USA and Canada
by Routledge
711 Third Avenue, New York, NY 10017

First issued in paperback 2014

Routledge is an imprint of the Taylor & Francis Group, an informa business

© 1942 George Routledge & Sons

British Library Cataloguing in Publication Data
A catalogue record for this book is available from the British Library

ISBN 13: 978-0-415-69699-9 (Volume 150)
ISBN 13: 978-1-138-00751-2 (pbk)

Publisher's Note
The publisher has gone to great lengths to ensure the quality of this reprint but points out that some imperfections in the original copies may be apparent.

Disclaimer
The publisher has made every effort to trace copyright holders and would welcome correspondence from those they have been unable to trace.

EDUCATION

A SEARCH FOR NEW PRINCIPLES

By

HERBERT PHILLIPSON

" The gods had much rather that mankind
should resemble than flatter them."

MARCUS AURELIUS.

GEORGE ROUTLEDGE & SONS LTD.

BROADWAY HOUSE, 68–74 CARTER LANE, E.C. 4

First published 1942

To

MILDRED

THIS BOOK IS PRODUCED IN COMPLETE
UNIFORMITY WITH THE AUTHORIZED
ECONOMY STANDARDS

Printed in Great Britain by T. and A. CONSTABLE LTD.
at the University Press, Edinburgh

CONTENTS

CHAPTER I

PHILOSOPHY AND SOCIAL PRACTICE

"Let our artists rather be those who are gifted to discern the true nature of the beautiful and graceful; then will our youth dwell in a land of health, amid fair sights and sounds, and receive the good of everything; and beauty, the effluence of fair works, shall flow into the eye and ear, like a health-giving breeze from a purer region, and insensibly draw the soul from earliest years into likeness and sympathy with the beauty of reason."—PLATO, *Republic*.

THE reader should be warned here and now that it is not intended either to use the Educational Philosophy of Plato as the foundation of workable Principles of Education for our times, or to hold up to our teachers and society, as an admonishment, the ideals of the Greeks to offset the failures of the present century. Either course would doubtless demand the respectful attention of many of our leaders of Educational thought, for their rise to the eminence of leadership in this branch of social philosophy often owes much to their knowledge and quotation of Plato, Aristotle and their followers. Not that there is anything against these ancient sages; as an expression of the highest ideals of contemporary Greek civilization the philosophy of Plato is as wise as it is beautiful.

Plato is chosen for no other reason than that his theory, which is diligently studied, at first or at second hand, by our teachers, contrasts so sharply with the realities of Education in practice. And this contrast demonstrates most clearly the need for the recognition, by educationists, of the essential interdependence of the social milieu and the contemporary theory and practice in Education.

From this point it will be possible to go forward to an examination of the results of this interdependence,

A

and from thence to determine new, and, it is hoped, workable Principles of Education.

The Educational Method of Plato, as described in the foregoing quotation (it would be well to read it again), is to surround the youth of his times with an environment in which moderation, order, harmony and courage are apparent on every side. He would even go so far as to arrange a censorship of words, rhythms, melodies and all sights and sounds which help to make up this environment. And his ultimate object is to "insensibly draw the soul from earliest years into likeness and sympathy with the beauty of reason."

What does such a method imply?

It suggests that in some of their relationships, economic, social or individual, the Greeks did not follow the precepts and example of their philosophers. There was, in fact, even in the age when Greek life seems to have been purest, a definite cleavage between philosophical precept and social practice. And this cleavage made necessary the seclusion of the youth from society during the period of its education.

Whether this method of education in a secluded and carefully ordered environment justified itself in the days of Plato and Aristotle is doubtful. That it produced many "good men" who approached the philosophers' ideal is certain. But whether it produced a "good" society through the precept and example of these "good men" is a more difficult question. For it must be remembered, first, that this was a slave civilization and only a small proportion of the slaves benefited by the education, and, secondly, that the golden age did not last long under the influence of the philosophers, for gradually the cleavage between precept and practice, in social and individual relations, became wider.

All that need be said now is that Greek ideals of virtue and goodness can have meaning only in so far, and so long, as they reflected the practical social and individual relationships within the community. After all, that is the ultimate practical test for any philosophy.

Can the methods of the Greeks, and their ideals of physical, moral and aesthetic education, help the teachers and educationists in our society? It is, of course, impracticable in our society completely to separate the children from outside influence during their period of education. To bring up a child in the complete seclusion of Plato's ordered environment, and then place him (be it never so gently) into the social life of our times, would be almost as disastrous, in its results, as removing a budding orchid from a hothouse into a snowstorm; the orchid certainly would not flower.

Even so, our educationists maintain that, following the broad principles of Plato and his disciples, much can be done in our schools to produce citizens who understand justice, truth and order, and whose virtues are strengthened by a knowledge and appreciation of beauty and reason. Unfortunately, the cleavage between philosophically accepted ideals and human behaviour, which was noticeable even in the Greek period at its best, has gradually become wider and wider. Methods of bridging this gap—now a gulf—vary in different civilizations and in different periods of history. At the time of Plato, to quote P. R. Cole [1]: "For the minority of the Greeks there was unity between theory and practice. They followed philosophy, but not religious precepts. . . . [These were far below the accepted philosophical standards.] . . . The principal safeguards of conduct were,

[1] *History of Educational Thought:* London, 1931, Oxford University Press.

in fact, law and custom, patriotism, the conception of moral nobility as eternal, the idea that pleasure accompanies the good life, a popular belief in Fate and the Furies, moral teaching based upon Homer and the theogony of Hesiod, a conception of family honour, a desire for fame after death, and a close supervision of the whole period of boyhood by trusted slaves called pedagogues."

This mixture of tradition, mythology and philosophy was only partially successful in maintaining the quality of Greek civilization. And this partial success did not last for long. Traditions are always in a state of conflict with the new activities and social relationships which inevitably accompany developments in the economic life of the community. Mythology may influence the behaviour of the group and the individual in ceremonial activities and seasonal occupations, but it rarely stands up for long against the expansive demands of trade and commerce. The philosophers, with their educational system, strove the harder to reinforce the bounds which tradition and mythology let loose.

The authority of religious precepts, which were modified to support the philosophical concepts of the "good" and the "beautiful," failed to increase, or even maintain, the influence of philosophy and education on social and individual behaviour. As this influence weakened, the great philosophers and teachers retired more and more into the seclusion of their academies, where their discussion and teaching became more complex and intangible and even less useful as a guide to the community outside.

So it was in ancient Greece: and so in Rome. It is difficult to reconcile the highest aspirations of Virgil and Livy, Tacitus, Pliny and Plutarch, with the social life in Rome when Augustus, Nero or Caligula were Emperors.

For the philosophers of these times seclusion was not enough; often safety lay only in silence.

Until the end of the fifteenth century the teachings of the ancient philosophers were lost to Western Europe. Under feudalism there had been no use for philosophy anyway, for, in the feudal community, personal relations were dictated by well-established economic relations. What education there was belonged to the monasteries and was almost exclusively religious. But by the sixteenth century the old feudalism had disappeared, and entirely new relationships, economic and social, soon established themselves. The distinction. between different classes of society was now real; the economic basis of this distinction included a form of competition which the feudal mind would never have understood—that is, the rivalry between individuals to obtain a livelihood by working, or by buying and selling the products of others' work.

But during this period of transition. Education gained a new meaning; for, from this time onwards, it became a necessity for a gradually increasing number of men to have some secular education. To read and write and calculate were important assets in the commercial age which was to follow.

It is reasonable to suppose that the new spirit of rivalry between individuals (which, of course, was not widespread until after the sixteenth century) resulted in the growth of new attitudes towards one's neighbour, and the modification of existing attitudes. Such emotional dispositions as, for example, jealousy, suspicion, hate and fear must have changed in quality—how completely we cannot judge—since the days of feudalism when the basic economic relationships which determined social behaviour were different.

In the great centres of learning, Oxford and Cambridge,

religion and classical philosophy ruled side by side. True, it was not a partnership on equal terms, yet the platonic ideals of beauty, truth and honour, and the rules of moderation, order and reason, were often adopted by the poets and dramatists and men of letters in place of the more purely Christian virtues. As long as the splendid nobility of Elizabeth's days maintained its stability the neo-platonic ideals showed their influence in the chivalry of the Court. But these ideals of virtue had not the same meaning for Sidney and Spenser as they had for Plato; they were accepted (and within narrow limits practised) as an embellishment, grafted upon a changed and changing basis of practical human relationships. The new "philosophers" did not examine the soil to see if it would feed the rare plant they had discovered. Once again Greek ideals, Christianized or not, failed to become a part of everyday social practice.

When a philosophical concept comes into sharp conflict with a changing system of practical human relationships, it can either retire into honourable seclusion as an "ideal" or accept patiently (I almost said "philosophically") the inevitable re-interpretation or modification by the more enlightened philosophers of the times.

After almost two hundred years of honourable retirement, the platonic "ideals" of beauty and virtuous action, sometimes taken from the original Greek writings, sometimes from a second-hand source like Spenser and Milton, were welcomed into the drawing-rooms of society once again.

From 1500 the great age of Geographical Discovery, from 1800 the great age of Scientific Discovery, brought within the comprehension of man vast new possibilities. In the first period the discovery of new sources of wealth, in the second the discovery of new forces by which to create wealth, liberated within humanity itself new springs of thought and action.

Perhaps those men who harnessed the newly discovered powers to machines needed a blend of romanticism, idealism and religion to help them forget the horror and degradation in the lives of their fellow-men who worked in the factories and mines. Keats, Shelley, Scott, Lamb, Wordsworth and Coleridge were products of this same society. Idealism, sentiment and sentimentality oozed from their essays, poetry and novels. The romanticism of the age, except in rare instances, passed over the classical rules of moderation, order and reason, and Art, whose social function should be to translate philosophy into popular form, sought beauty in intangibility, reason in mysticism, and justice only in the heavens above.

The cleavage between religion and philosophy on the one hand, and the practical relationship of man with man on the other, was almost complete. It was easier to persuade man to lament the captivity of an ass,[1] or the destruction of a tree,[2] than it was to persuade him

[1] Coleridge : " To a Young Ass."

> " Poor little foal of an oppressed race !
> I love the languid patience of thy face :
> And oft with gentle hand I give thee bread,
> And clap thy ragged coat, and pat thy head. . . .
>
> .   .   .   .   .
>
> Or is thy sad heart thrill'd with filial pain
> To see thy wretched mother's shorten'd chain ?
> And truly, very piteous is her lot,—
> Chain'd to a log within a narrow spot,
> Where the close-eaten grass is scarcely seen,
> While sweet around her waves the tempting green."
>
> (From *Poems* 1796.)

[2] Wordsworth : " Nutting."

> " Ere from the mutilated bower I turned
> Exulting, rich beyond the wealth of kings,
> I felt a sense of pain when I beheld
> The silent trees, and saw the intruding sky. . . ."   (1799.)

of the human nature and consequent rights of all his fellow-men.

While the exuberance and vitality of the writers and poets at the beginning of the nineteenth century recall the spirit of wonder and expectancy in Elizabethan literature, the almost complete severance of art from the broad masses of society in the later age is significant. The Elizabethan people clung to drama, folk music and poetry as their own, as an expression of their consciousness and joy in living. (Beside this art, the poetry and novels of the narrow Court circle show superficiality and false ornamentation.) But the joy and vitality of the Romantics, in spite of all the efforts of the "Lyrical Ballad" poets, did not express a kindred feeling in the hearts of the people who lived through the first decades of the Industrial Revolution.

Like Rousseau, Wordsworth applauded the idea of educating man according to the example and laws of nature.[1] He disliked the new society of the towns.[2] In the first flush of enthusiasm for Rousseau's rights of the individual, Wordsworth supported the French Revolution,[3] but, failing to understand what this great social upheaval really meant, he retired, at the thought of bloodshed, to the soothing seclusion of the Lakes. Henceforward his poetic mind could only face the city at night.[4]

Keats and Shelley [5] were equally unaware of the real significance of the Industrial Revolution, and because they had little practical contact with the masses of the people their contribution to social consciousness was very

[1] In " The Prelude."
[2] Compare " Michael " and " The Prelude "—Book Seven, etc.
[3] " Bliss is it in this dawn to be alive."
[4] Sonnet on Westminster Bridge.
[5] Shelley's outcries against social injustice rarely find a place in anthologies of his poems.

slight. Their art was for man in isolation, for it expressed nothing of the practical relationship of man with man.

> ". . . Oh why should I
> Feel cursed and thwarted when the liegeless air
> Yields to my step aspirant? Why should I
> Spurn the green turf as hateful to my feet?
> Goddess benign! point forth some unknown thing,
> Are there not other regions than this isle?
> What are the stars? There is the sun, the sun!
>
> .   .   .   .   .
>
> I have heard the cloudy thunder: Where is power?
> Whose hand, whose essence, what divinity
> Makes this alarum in the Elements,
> While I here idle listen on the shores
> In fearless yet in aching ignorance?
> Knowledge enormous makes a God of me,
> Names, deeds, grey legends, dire events, rebellions,
> Majesties, sovran voices, agonies,
> Creations and destroyings, all at once
> Pour into the wide hollows of my brain,
> And deify me, as if some blithe wine,
> Or bright elixir peerless I had drunk
> And so become immortal."

("Hyperion.")

The influence of Rousseau did not basically affect the philosophical attitude of the nineteenth century. Plato had claimed the right and the authority to mould human nature, without taking into consideration the dynamic interrelation between social environment and human behaviour. His ideals would work, therefore, only *in vacuo*. And that is precisely where they did continue to function; in the minds of philosophers and poets, but rarely in the actions of social man.

Now, Rousseau demanded the complete freedom of the individual to develop according to the laws of nature; by which he usually meant the innate nature of man. He had much to contribute to the service of Education in some of his suggestions, such as: "Nature would have children be children before being men," and in his request to his tutors to substitute well-regulated liberty for the ordinary educational instruments of "emulation, jealousy, envy, vanity, covetousness and debasing fear." But his emphasis on human nature, the unchanging and unchangeable inborn nature of man, as the key to education for citizenship, shows that his philosophical attitude has the same shortcoming as that of Plato and his disciples. He failed to recognize the essential inter-relationship between the social milieu and the contemporary mind. "Emulation, jealousy, envy, vanity, covetousness and debasing fear" were to Rousseau the inevitable concomitant of social life, especially in the cities. That these qualities attached themselves to human nature, thriving in this special social milieu of the cities, did not lead him to examine the why or the wherefore of such a phenomenon. "Man is naturally good, but socially depraved," and that is the end of it.

At the end of *Emile*, Rousseau can say: "Here is the good man, shown as he emerges through the formative processes of education. The Good State will be that which offers him scope and opportunity and sets up no conflict between his civil duty and his moral judgment." Rousseau's idea, then, was the education of the unchanging nature of man for life in a State which he knew did not exist.

The task of the present day is to educate the changed and changing nature of the child in relation to a new social milieu which we know can exist, and which we will plan consciously and scientifically. In building this new society the child will play his part, for it is his heritage that we plan to build. Mistakes will be made, but they will be recognized and remedied as they become apparent. "Truth comes more readily out of error than out of confusion," wrote Bacon, and confusion can result only from wrong premises.

Here are the children; here our world with all its wealth and power and beauty; and here too the sum of countless ages of toil, experience and thought; enough of knowledge to wrest from our world the food for life and enjoyment. The interrelation between these three prime factors has gone wrong; we must examine why, and if, like many a scientist, we find error has accumulated upon error, for long-accepted premises were wrong, we must face the toil of reconstruction cheerfully, for the future is at stake.

CHAPTER II

THE SCHOOL AND THE SOCIAL ENVIRONMENT

WHEN people are confronted with obvious contradictions between principle and practice in our society they usually react in one or more of these ways:

Some express a violent, unreasoned antagonism towards the unfortunate human being who has drawn their attention to the contradiction. This reaction has much in common with the way a patient reacts to the clinical psychologist when he suggests the real, but unconscious, causes of behaviour.

Others dismiss the contradiction as an inevitable and unchangeable state of affairs which owes its origin to forces completely beyond human control.

A few—benevolent and bewhiskered—content themselves by saying, "Look what has been done to improve the situation; it takes time, you know." It is only a short step from this attitude to that of the teacher (now retired) who pointed out that it was not necessary to agitate for smaller classes in our schools, for the declining birth-rate would solve the problem for us in time!

And yet a great many adopt the attitude of Ratty in "The Wild Wood"[1]: hardship, hunger, danger, and maybe death are just around the corner, but it is bad form to speak of it; for to be constantly reminded of such unpleasant eventualities spoils one's appetite. I remember a President of the National Union of Teachers making all these excuses at once when I presented him with a press article in which I had pointed out that a Government Grant, covering all the requirements to make the 1936 Education Act work, would cost the nation less

---

[1] *Wind in the Willows*, by Kenneth Grahame : London, Methuen.

each year than the next war would cost each day. Against the President's advice, I submitted the article to the Editor of the local newspaper; it was accepted, except for the financial comparison which the Editor blue-pencilled, casually observing, "The Public don't like such comparisons, you know."

There is at the present time a deep and widespread consciousness that our Educational system is not satis-factory. After the war this consciousness will seek to translate itself into planning and action. And there is plenty of evidence that the people of Britain will not be satisfied with a patched-up system of Education any more than they will be satisfied with a patched-up Peace. They will welcome an examination of fundamentals when the time comes to plan the reconstruction of our social, economic and political life. The realities of the war have come too close to be idealized and they have struck too deeply to be forgotten. The social consciousness of the people has been shaken as never before. They have experienced disillusionment and distrust. These feelings still linger, no longer in relation to the future, but pro-jected upon past forms and traditions, and upon those members of society who still defend them.

With the invasion of Soviet Russia came hope.

But the magnificent defence of the Soviet Union not only surprised the general public by revealing the real strength of organization and resources in this "Back-ward" country, it showed and continues to show the fine texture of a civilization which had hitherto been misrepresented and misunderstood, and it provided the peoples in the Democracies with the opportunity of finding out the true nature of Soviet ideals and achievements.

Hope became stronger as admiration grew. The tremendous sacrifices, the tremendous faith and the unbreakable unity of the Soviet peoples has given to the people of Britain a new meaning for their own struggle. It has opened up in the minds of many the possibility of a new social order after the war, and it is the right to build this new society which they are fighting for.

Our view of the Soviet Russia at war is less distorted than was our view of the Soviets at peace, and there has resulted in our midst a wave of self-criticism against which propaganda dare no longer train its loudest guns. For it is now apparent that:

(a) The Soviet people are not uncivilized.

(b) The Soviet Government does not persecute religion.

(c) They may have omitted, in some instances, to fit bath plugs, but on the whole their industrial organization must be fairly efficient.

(d) (And this is most astonishing to the prejudiced mind) The 160,000,000 members of the Soviet Union have demonstrated an unshakable faith in their new civilization.

True criticism must begin with self-criticism. The courage to admit that long-established theories, attitudes and traditions may have led civilization astray is the first necessity in planning a new world after the war. This will be a new quality of courage, for it will owe its strength to a faith in human ability, and to a deep love of humanity, and it will attain its success from an understanding born of unprejudiced investigation. The search for new Principles for Education cannot be undertaken without such courage. The first task is to examine the present condition of Education with special reference to such Principles as are generally accepted.

Every teacher has a vague recollection of books on "Principles of Education" and "Educational Thought," which had to be read during the period of training. After only a few years of teaching there remains, of this reading and study, little in the mind of the teacher save the title of a "Set Book." All those chapters on "Training of the Emotions," "Nature and Nurture," "Discipline," "Suggestion," "The Adolescent," etc., etc., which at the time of reading seemed full of inspiration and possibilities, are remembered only as headings, or definitions or, more vaguely, as "Ideals." The teacher, looking back on the enthusiasm of his Training Centre days, often laughs at the credulity which allowed him to build his hopes upon such foundations. And, as a teacher of experience, he will adopt a somewhat superior air, when these forgotten authorities are quoted, and say, "Well, we have not the time to bother with these ideas nowadays; they're all right in a book, you know; in any case they won't work in a school, you can take it from me." If pressed to say why they won't work in the school, the answer will invariably include references to: home conditions, size of classes, school accommodation, lack of equipment, discipline, the influence of the cinema and the nature of the child.

The teacher is quite right; the Principles of Education, which seemed so full of insight and promise, yield a very poor return in actual teaching practice. The astonishing fact, however, is that teachers and educationists generally accept this sorry state of affairs as a natural condition. The Principles are looked upon as Ideals, and Ideals are looked down upon as "something unattainable, anyway."

The more we examine our Educational practice, the more apparent it becomes that there are no practical guiding Principles to direct the efforts of our teachers. This is admitted by Dr. F. H. Spencer in his recent book *Education for the People*.[1] He points out that there is no

---

[1] London, 1941, George Routledge & Sons.

philosophy, no principle upon which our Educational curriculum and teaching are based, and that we are, in fact, just "gropers."

In building up a philosophy, as in constructing a theory in the practical sciences, there is always the need to refer back to fundamentals; it is not enough to develop the accepted theory in the light of new knowledge and experimental observation. There came a time in history when it was necessary to recognize that the earth is round, for the old, long-accepted idea that it is flat was obstructing further scientific progress.

We have reached a like stage in Educational progress at this present time. It is clear that something is holding back Educational progress. Much has been done in a haphazard kind of way to reduce the size of classes in our schools, to improve school buildings, to provide more and better equipment, to supervise the physical welfare of the children, and to ensure that Secondary Education is accessible to the poorer families. Much more needs to be done, the quicker the better, but these improvements cannot of themselves solve the Educational problem.

Education must be a social activity; it must be a dynamic part of the social life of the whole community. If it is not that, then the forces of Education, centred in our schools, will inevitably expend themselves with little result, in face of the practical examples of the social milieu outside. If the principles which determine activity within the school are in conflict with those principles which determine the practical social relationships in the whole community, then Education must be unsatisfactory, and the results will be far behind possibilities.

"Education must, it would seem, be limited to securing for every one the conditions under which individuality is most completely developed—that is, to enable him to make his original contribution to the variegated whole of human life as full and as truly characteristic as his nature permits." [1]

How does this work out in actual practice? Consider first the problem of "securing for every child the conditions under which individuality is most completely developed."

For five years I worked in a school which served a very poor district in one of our larger cities. It was originally a Church School; the accommodation was deplorable—two or even three classes in one room, very bad lighting, no room for special subjects, and an asphalt playground no bigger than a chicken-run. There I taught some of the finest boys in the country—and, of course, some of the most difficult cases too. Comparing the school with others which served more prosperous sections of the community, I found that the percentage of boys with more than average intelligence was slightly lower, and the percentage of dull, backward and difficult cases definitely higher, in the poorer school. These results were confirmed by the use of standardized Intelligence Tests, Achievement Tests and Subject Tests.

What were the chief factors involved? The poor condition of the school and its lack of space and equipment were a definite handicap in spite of the efforts of an excellent staff. True, the limitations imposed by the school premises often made the teachers curse Local Authorities and all other responsible bodies, but the school itself was not responsible for our greatest handicap. It was never impossible to create the means and space for developing the individuality of the boys; every possible form of interest and self-expression had our practical sympathy. Yet there was always the world

---

[1] *Education, its Data and First Principles*, by P. Nunn : London, 1930, Arnold.

B

outside, undermining every effort we and the children made. It was never just the home, or the parents, or the street, or the cinema which did the damage; it was the whole pattern of social life around, which wove itself imperceptibly into the child's consciousness, obscuring the real purpose of his school activities, misdirecting his finer impulses, and trampling his ambitions.

I remember all these boys; seven years of their lives they came to this school, and for five years I knew them all.

There was Fuss, the unquestionable genius who had shown as much, if not more, artistic ability than our art master (one of the best in the city), and whose personality and self-confidence made him the leader—and at times the master—of the school. Where is he now? Did he not win a scholarship to some College of Art, you ask. Easily, but he did not go. He became first an errand boy, later the odd-job man with some back-street painter and paper-hanger.

Then there was Jimmy who never seemed to grow. He was full of life and fun; a boy of more than average intelligence and in addition very painstaking and a great reader. What did our school make of Jimmy? A page boy at the local cinema: when he becomes sixteen another will take his place.

And George, whose all-round abilities might have gained him a Tripos and a Blue. When last I saw him he was an errand boy, pushing a huge wooden box in front of his bicycle.

And Wilf, whose father was always out of work. For months he came late to school; never very dirty, but invariably most untidy and bleary-eyed. His mother annoyed me intensely by choosing practice nights and Saturday mornings to send him on her most urgent errands. Very good at mathematics, Wilf came nearly top of the entrance examination to the Technical College. The day after he should have started there the Principal of the College 'phoned our Headmaster to see why Wilf had not turned up. We sent to his home for him, and soon he appeared in the raggiest possible pants and shirt, yet surprisingly clean. He had been afraid to go to the Technical College in his dirty clothes, so he had washed his only pair of raggy flannels and attempted to mend them. The result was most unfortunate; they were just unwearable. A few days later we sent him off with decent clothes, gym and football kit, and strict instructions to come and see us very often. For a whole term Wilf did very well. Where is he now? First he stole a bicycle, then he borrowed a car, and they transferred Wilf to a Borstal Institution during my summer holidays.

Young Eddie turned out one of the most difficult boys in the school. Like his brother before him, and the little one who is following after, he was at first most likeable and well dispositioned. I remember Eddie winning my class prize when he was about eleven; how he read and re-read that copy of *Dog Crusoe*, bestowing on the book all the care and attention he would have bestowed on the dog itself, could he have had it. Yet what a falling-off was there before he left school. For four shillings a week he delivered papers before and after school. He aspired to long trousers and joined the "gang" his brother had formed. Six nights each week were spent at the "pictures." Where is he now? I just don't know.

And Mac, a fascinating lad, dirty, ragged and generally very sleepy. Intelligence, just average. One Christmas holiday I went with a colleague to deliver a new (second-hand) suit and a shirt at his home. We found a drunken grandfather, a bare floor, some broken chairs and the filthy remains of many meals on the bare table. Mac was out. I remembered that afternoon that Mac had only a few weeks before executed a very commendable illustration of the poem "The Elfin Artist." What right had I to attempt to guide his appreciation of the beautiful? What could he know of "glades," and "hare-bells," and "dew," and "the light in the blackbird's eye"? What happened to Mac? God knows. I hope he won through.

Dozens of bright personalities crowd across my mind as I write of these boys. Each smiles gratefully and intimately as when I meet them in the streets. Could we have helped them better than we did? Maybe. But their education was never anything but a patchwork of inventions which threw bright lights across their path, then left them stranded in the blackout where they live.

Was it the home, or the condition of the school? I do not think so, for when the old school closed down I was fortunate enough to be transferred to a fine new Senior Boys' School which served the housing estate where many of my former pupils now lived. There I found the same boys—or their fellows from adjacent slums. Now they lived in semi-detached houses, with large gardens and plenty of space around. The school provided all that could be desired in space, playing fields, gymnasium, subject rooms and equipment. And certainly the changed environment brought forth results, if slowly. Health and cleanliness improved. The interests of the boys became more varied and generally keener. Yet still our education failed. The new environment was basically the same as the old. The customs, habits, social attitudes and interests of the housing-estate community may, in time, show a measure of refinement over the old slum communities, but that will be all. Competition, rivalry, greed, distrust, hate, apathy, fear and despair are rooted in the whole social system. Work has become a meaningless imposition; pleasure an escape from the uncertainties and insecurities of everyday life. Nothing can bind the community together into real meaningful activity in the world outside school; and the world inside school adopts an entirely separate and unrelated system of precepts and examples.

Did we try "Training of the Emotions"? From Plato unto Cavenagh we tried. Moderation, order and beauty in colour, shape and sound were for ever before the children inside school. With what result? Instead of our efforts "insensibly drawing the soul from earliest years into a likeness and sympathy with the beauty of reason," the practical example of the social milieu drew the children from earliest years into the likeness and sympathy with the ugliness of unreason. True, the boys came to enjoy music, poetry, art and modelling as a luxury which existed inside schools, art galleries—and more rarely in the privacy of a room at home. Yet they knew only too well that moderation, order, beauty and reason have very little part in the practical social relationships of the world they have to live in.

Did we try "Moral Teaching"? We did, right reverend sir—too much of it! Let no parson ever moan to me that juvenile delinquency is due to lack of "moral training." Let him first find out what "moral training" really is. Let him help to set right the foundations of our social life, so that his Christ is not crucified in the daily life of every child. If "moral training" and social practice are in conflict, it would be only wise to examine the social practice as well as the "moral training."

And were the inspectors pleased with our work in the old school and the new? Most definitely so; the plays the boys produced on the tiny stage in the old school hall, the bookbinding, posters, fretwork, poetry illustrations, diaries, scrap books, news sheets, magazines and debates all pleased their little minds. They showed that the artificial life of the school trained useful skills and tastes and talents in the boys. But what of the world outside? Of George and Eddie, Fuss and Wilf and Mac, and hundreds of their fellows, when they packed away their books, pens, saws, brushes, stage properties and smiles to leave the school for work?

"Let us train our children to face the complicated problems of life cheerfully and resourcefully; let us try to give them the self-confidence to examine and construct"—as useless as setting a mousetrap to catch a German tank. Why must we try to train in the child those qualities of virtue and social strength which our community cannot or dare not grasp for itself? The cleavage between Educational Theory and Social Practice cannot be bridged in this way; the two are interdependent, and the responsibility of society is clear.

For this is a society which attempts to train its children to enjoy all the possibilities that life now offers, yet safeguards the right to full enjoyment for a small minority of the population. It is a society which professes to follow the Christian teachings and to pass them on to its children, yet which allows every Christian tenet to be violated in its fundamental human relationship; a society which holds fast to

yet ignores
"Thou shalt not steal"

"Thou shalt not exploit."

It is a civilization which trains the child to enjoy the beauty of our world and all that grows and lives thereon; yet which permits the wanton destruction of these beauties in war and peaceful profit-grabbing.

In short, it is a civilization bold enough and sufficiently hypocritical to persuade itself that its children can be taught to believe what their elders do not practise.

CHAPTER III

THE NATURE OF ENVIRONMENT

"Man is naturally good, but socially depraved."—ROUSSEAU.

"The nature of the child must determine all the details of his Education."—PESTALOZZI.

"Let us get a clear idea of what the primary business of Education is. The child has to learn to control its instincts. . . . The function of Education, therefore, is to inhibit, forbid and suppress, and it has at all times carried out this function to admiration."—FREUD.

"The whole of history is nothing but the progressive transformation of human nature."—MARX.

THE same attitudes are adopted towards our Educational problems as are current in relation to the Rise of Fascism, Unemployment, Depressions and the present World War. We either blame the nature of the individual or we blame the uncontrollable influences at work in the world around.

Either way is to refuse to recognize the obvious and essential grounds of investigation and experiment. If it is taken for granted—

(a) that the nature of the individual is responsible for our social ills, and that this nature is unchangeable, and in certain respects unknowable;

and

(b) that mankind can be involved in social attitudes and activities by reason of influences over which he has no control;

then we have confusion struggling against confusion, and the only result can be confusion more confounded.

Our knowledge, which is continually increasing, has set at the disposal of mankind ever greater funds of necessities and sources of enjoyment; yet as an excuse for our mismanagement of these resources, we postulate that the unchangeable nature of man includes vicious animal impulses which all our knowledge cannot control; or we say that our organization of the production and distribution of these resources produces conditions which are beyond explanation and control.

The nature of man and the nature of environment are the two fundamentals of social philosophy, and any search for new principles of Education must start with an examination of these fundamentals.

It will, of course, be impossible to consider the two separately. There is not any factor in environment, or in the nature of man, which can be isolated and examined by itself. Man biological and man psychological cannot be separated. Neither can the biological and psychological man be separated from his historic environment. The state of the environment in every detail depends on the men and women who live in that environment, and it is equally true to say that every activity of man, physical, emotional and psychological, depends upon his relationship with his environment.

Between man and his environment there is, then, an interrelationship, wherein no factors, or groups of factors, on either side, remain constant. The History of Mankind is nothing more than a record of the interrelation of man and his environment.

The two processes, the development of homo sapiens and the changing of environment, are not parallel, nor are they just related at certain points in some haphazard kind of way; they are interdependent, and the slightest change in the one affects the other at every point.[1]

---

[1] Compare Luria, *Nature of Human Conflicts* :

"Speech and the use of signs, the permutation of activity by the use of cultural means, make the human being a new biological species in history. These new functions do not remain isolated in the psychological process, but permeate the whole activity and structure of behaviour, so that we find them literally in every movement of the fingers."

Every gardener knows that a flower will not be exactly the same a second blossoming time as it was the first, be he never so careful to keep the conditions the same. The environment in which the plant was reared and that in which it blossomed first has changed, in some degree, the nature of the plant. Only in so far as the gardener understands the interdependence of plant and environment can he control the results of his labour. And on a very different level the future of the human species depends upon man's understanding of the species, individually and collectively, and its historic environment.

Such a philosophy demands a strictly materialist attitude to all phenomena. Yet it liberates, as the first fruit of its acceptance, far greater forces in the mind of man than did ever any Romantic Revival of the past. For it loosens the bounds which mankind has imposed upon his own mind, and for the first time in history it makes man the master of his own destiny.

It has been pointed out, in the first section of this essay, that the change from feudalism to the period of wage-earning and profit-making resulted in great changes in the social behaviour of mankind. In the feudal age economic and social relationships were one and the same thing. The fellowship which men shared one with the other had the most solid and essential of foundations—labour—the purpose of which was personal to every individual and never remote from the activity in which he shared.

During the centuries of work and wages which followed the gradual breakdown of feudal relationships, mankind has been separated, in ever-increasing degree, from the essential purpose of his labour: which purpose is, of course, to win from his environment as much of the world's resources as necessity and enjoyment demand.

The rapid increase in knowledge from the sixteenth century onwards was used to obscure this true purpose, rather than to bring about its realization. From that period to the present day, the means of changing the world's resources into usable commodities have become more firmly the private property of individuals and groups of individuals. And their main purpose has been, almost exclusively, to secure this property for themselves, for its possession guarantees a most liberal share of the necessities and enjoyments of life.

The result of such social activity on the part of these owners of the means of production must be obvious to a disinterested enquirer.

In the first place, there must be two distinct sections in the community—the owners of the means of production and distribution, and those who enter into the activity of producing but own neither the means they employ nor the goods they make. And, therefore, there can be no real unity of purpose behind the economic activities of the community as a whole.

Then again, a society so divided in its fundamental activities tends to lose all consciousness of the purpose of these activities. For owner and wage-earner alike, the activity of planning or of producing breeds no feeling of fellowship, but rather feelings of distrust, fear, apprehension and hate. The employer must control the longings of the employee, and the employee must be aware, be it only subconsciously, of the power which binds him.

It is the fashion to assert that these attitudes do not really exist in our society; but, given the economic basis, it is inevitable that they do exist; and their recognition cannot fail to explain the curious obstructions which, from time to time, hold up Educational progress. The much quoted administrator who, around 1860, shouted, "We must educate our masters," may have meant it, but the eighty years of Educational progress since that time has only succeeded in answering T. S. Eliot's prayer :

"Teach us to think, and not to think,
Teach us to sit still."

But the most significant effect of our present economic system is the negative attitude towards labour and the products of labour. Perhaps the word "impersonal" better describes this attitude. Imagine a social group, freely participating in the planning and producing of something which satisfies a conscious need in the group, and which, when produced, will become the property of the whole group, each member sharing in its amenities by right of his labour. Then consider, in contrast, the meaning of economic activity in our society: the wage-earner, who sells his labour to the owner of a factory, enters into the activity of producing with the main object of securing his wages: he may prefer one type of activity to another, according to his interests and abilities, yet his attitude towards his work and the products of his work must be largely "impersonal." The machinery and tools are the jealously guarded property of the factory owners; the raw material used in the factory evokes no feelings of fellowship with the workers who provided it; the goods, when made, pass into an "impersonal" market over which the worker has no control. And so with the owner of the means of production; the value of the labour he buys is calculated in terms of the "impersonal" market where the finished goods must be sold; the raw materials and commodities produced have no other significance than "market value"—that is the profit-making value.

During the last century the intricacies of Industry

and Commerce have resulted in a widening of the gap between the real and the actual value of commodities and the labour used in producing them. The greatest source of strength in a society—community of purpose, based upon community of labour—is completely lacking in our economic organization. Man works alone for his own ends, and he feels isolated from his fellow-workmen. He uses "impersonal" tools and machines in an "impersonal" factory, making thereby "impersonal" goods which are destined for an "impersonal" market. In return for his "impersonal" labour he receives "impersonal" wages.

Not only is man thus isolated in the basic social activity, but, by the nature of the organization, he is in conflict with his fellow-men. The one section of the community must secure work for wages in competition with their fellows, and the other section must secure the means and opportunity for making profit in competition with other profit-makers. In both sections of the community there is an ever-increasing competition for the opportunity to work or to make profit, and, therefore, there is a strengthening of those feelings of conflict which largely determine social relationships. At the same time, the inevitable state of tension which exists between wage-earners and profit-makers becomes more marked.

Because man cannot be conscious of a real purpose behind his productive activity, and because this activity is carried on in strict isolation, enforced by the necessities inherent in the whole economic organization, man not only works *alone*, but he also feels *alone*. He has become an individualist in the worst sense of the word, and his emotional attitude, in so far as it relates to his work as a wage-earner or as a profit-earner, is essentially selfish. Intensified competition in the labour market and in the selling market has made such an outlook an economic necessity for almost every individual.

Strangely enough, mankind cannot visualize a form of society in which selfishness, and the kindred attitudes of jealousy, hate, fear and aggression, do not exist. And he is equally incapable of visualizing any system of economic organization other than that in which he lives. The answer, of course, is quite simple. The strongest and most resistant emotional attitudes are those which are basically related to man's economic activity. These attitudes have been consolidated through long centuries wherein the same basic economic relationships have developed. The necessities of the economic organization have so interpenetrated with the mind of man that the resulting emotional dispositions have become an essential part of his *nature*—essential so long as he needs to live as a part of the present economic structure. For the very permanence of these attitudes is dependent upon the continuation of the economic system which gave them birth, just as the continuation of our economic organization is dependent upon the strength of the emotional attitudes which it fosters. In other words, the two fundamentals are interrelated and interdependent.

It is clear, then, that many emotional dispositions, common in our social life, are dependent, for their essential quality, upon the economic organization in which every individual plays some part. Admittedly, the high ideals of philosophy and religious teaching qualify these emotional dispositions. With some individuals these ideals may become realized in special instances of social practice, but, for the mass of humanity, this cannot be; neither philosopher nor parson can change the *nature* of our people, for this *nature* is the historic endowment of our peculiar form of economic organization. What Philosophy, Religion and Education can do is to provide a moral code which holds in check the anti-social attitudes which the economic organization fosters. Such a moral code is always in conflict with the *natural* dispositions of mankind, and all that can result from its teaching is a new system of dispositions, which the individual adopts, on top of, and separate from, the system of dispositions which have become *natural.* The latter persist in business life, political life and economic relations generally. The former, except in rare instances, are reserved for purely personal relationships.

Yet there cannot be a complete separation between economic and personal life in any society. It is absurd to suppose that the mind of man can so divide itself. Every thought and every emotion and every action of man in society must bear the imprint of the *nature* of man peculiar to that society. In short, however strong the influence of philosophy and religion, the economic structure of our society produces and maintains a *nature* in the individual which will change the quality of such influence or completely override it.

And this will always be the case as long as there is a cleavage between philosophy and the practical human relationships in society. Philosophy must be constructed from the most accurate and most advanced scientific examination of the basic relationships: these are,—the resources of man's mind and the resources of the world, as they are practically available and useful at any time in history. But philosophy cannot guide mankind from a position which is isolated from the practical life of the community: and it is useless if it is a static theory or ideal; it must be a dynamic and practical synthesis of knowledge. Philosophy must be the enlightened expression of the highest possibilities of human consciousness at any stage of historical development. And it must continually check itself from an examination of the social practice of which it is the highest expression.

What then is the function of Art in society? All men cannot be philosophers, for only the few are capable of the comprehensive study philosophy demands. Nor can all philosophers be artists, for philosophy is a science, and scientific thought and analysis does not always lend itself to direct artistic expression. Besides, the function of Art is to give pleasure, whatever form it uses. Philosophy expresses itself only in words; demanding the practical application of its achievements, it appeals mainly to the intellectual mind of man. The artist, by his dramatic representation of human relationships, invites the active and whole-hearted participation of the whole world in his art, as he gives meaning to human behaviour and points out to his vast audience new powers within themselves and new points of contact with the mother earth. The supreme function of the artist, then, is to express in a popular and understandable form the highest possibilities of progress for his age.

But such philosophers and such artists do not, and cannot, exist in our present society.[1] The economic structure calls for other services from our thinkers and artists. Theirs is a task most necessary and most useful; it is to explain away or excuse the more obvious contrasts between what does exist and what is presumed to exist, between apparent beauty and disguised ugliness, between fine sentiments and foul deeds, between man's knowledge and the achievements thereof, between a love of peace and an inevitable war, in short, between accepted theory and unacceptable practice.

[1] See Appendix I.

CHAPTER IV

THE NATURE OF THE INDIVIDUAL

But, it will be asked, what of the biological nature of man? It is surely beyond the influences of the social and economic environment? In the present state of biological knowledge, it would certainly be difficult to demonstrate that the organs, tissues and glandular secretions in the human body change with the changing environment. What can be done is to examine the "quality" of human behaviour in different patterns of society, for the behaviour of the individual or the community as a whole is, after all, the thing which really matters. The biological, the social and the psychological in mankind are interrelated at every point, and the results of these interrelationships have meaning only in the behaviour of the individual or social group.

It is unfortunate that most anthropologists have failed to recognize the economic basis of the patterns of culture which they have observed and described. Their attitude to their subjects is very much like that of our present-day historians; they connect only attitudes and activities, and for the origin of these attitudes they are content to point out the nature of the individual or group, or the nature of the environment.

From the descriptive work of such modern anthropologists as Stefansson, Malinowski, Fortune and Ruth Benedict it is possible to understand something of the quality of the emotional attitudes which exist in primitive societies. In every society so far examined the *repellent* emotional attitudes which we describe as jealousy, fear and hate, and the *attractive* emotional attitudes which we describe as sympathy, confidence and love, are shown in the behaviour of the people. Yet it is a grave mistake to suppose that these emotional dispositions have the same quality as those we describe by the use of the same words in our society. The quality of emotion, like the true meaning of words, cannot be accurately translated from one community to another. Experience of the emotion, and of the use of words, is necessary for their complete understanding, and this experience must be as an active member of the community. It is manifestly easier to understand the language of a people whose pattern of culture is similar to one's own—for example, the western European peoples—than it is to understand the full content of verbal expression amongst a people whose economic, social and cultural life has developed separately and upon a different basis.

To describe the emotional attitudes and the behaviour of primitive peoples who have had little or no contact with western civilization is the most hazardous task of all. For the mind of the anthropologist is essentially and inseparably related to his own environment—and so is the content of every word he uses in describing his observations in a strange milieu. A long and unbroken contact with the strange pattern of culture and an active participation in the everyday life of the community may help the anthropologist to understand something of the *nature* of the pattern, yet any attempt to pass on this understanding to westerners must introduce into the minds of his readers those very errors which, by years of field work, he had partly removed from his own mind. Our language is a social and historical product, and by its use we convey meaning only in so far as the social and historical content is familiar.

The behaviour of primitive peoples, as described by anthropologists, does show the existence of *repellent* and *attractive* attitudes, but when our words "jealousy,"

c

"hate," "fear," "sympathy," "love," etc., are used to describe these attitudes, we must seek the content of the words, not in our own experience, but in the social milieu in which the behaviour was observed. That repellent and attractive emotional attitudes are experienced by people in every pattern of culture so far examined does not mean that human *nature* is the same, in any respect, the world over. The quality of the attitudes, and the purpose and meaning of the consequent behaviour, is a function of the social and historical development of a particular community in a particular geographical setting. "The history of mankind is nothing more than the progressive transformation of human nature," and, in the history of mankind, geography plays a vital part.

An Eskimo may show no feeling of "jealousy" if his mate is intimate with another man, yet the same Eskimo will be profoundly distressed, jealous and angry if his mate deserts him just before or during the hunting season. At this season she is necessary to him not just as a wife, but as a helper in preparing and executing all the duties connected with successful hunting expeditions; and an unsuccessful hunting season will mean hardship, hunger and even starvation in the Arctic winter. It is obvious that the reactions of the Eskimo are different in quality from those which we describe by the use of the same words, "jealousy," "hate," "aggression" and the like. The reactions depend for their quality upon the social milieu in which the Eskimos live, and the whole of their social and individual behaviour has meaning only within that specific milieu.

It is impossible to extract the *nature* of the Eskimo from the social setting wherein Stefansson made his observations. Nor is the *nature* of the Mexican Indian, the Melanesian or the Australian Aborigine the same *nature* in disguise. The truth is that the *nature* of man is not a thing in itself, and it does not exist apart from a definite social and historical environment.[1]

In some of the Melanesian Islands there is, or was, a ceremonial trading of food between the fisher folk and the yam growers. At the recognized seasons the former carry, as a gift, the best of their catch to the natives who live inland. A return expedition is then arranged, when those who live inland bring their choicest yams and fruits to the fisher folk. There is abundance of produce in these islands and there is no rivalry for the possession of these essential commodities. The only rivalry which does exist is in the growing of yams or in the catching of fish, for it is accounted a great honour to provide the choicest and best for the ceremonial gift. This rivalry exists not only for the sake of the ceremonial feast, but in almost all the productive occupations of the natives.[2] And there is evidence that the emotional impulses which result occasionally lead to misunderstandings—and even acts of aggression. But here again it is misleading to use our language to describe the social and individual relationships which characterize the behaviour of these people. "Fear," "jealousy," "hate," "aggression," or "sympathy," "admiration," "love" are words which have a special meaning in our pattern of culture. Their

[1] Compare V. Stefansson, *My Life with the Eskimo*, page 149 :

" Commonly, primitive peoples are supposed to have certain mental qualities, designated as ' instinctive,' through which they vastly excel us along certain lines, and to make up for the excellence they are supposed to be far our inferiors in certain other mental characteristics. My own observations incline me to believe that there are no points in which they, as a race, are any more inferior to us than might be expected from the environment under which they have grown up from childhood, and neither have they any points of superiority over the white man, except those which are developed directly by the environment."

[2] *Op. cit.*, page 269. See Appendix II for extract.

associations, as we use the words, would be incomprehensible to people who are a part of a different social pattern. And in every case the attitudes these words describe can be classified only from an observation of the behaviour of individuals or social groups in relation to their fellow-men. Because we observe that there is rivalry, or even antagonism between individuals or communities in these primitive civilizations, we cannot postulate that emotional dispositions of a like quality to our own determine their behaviour.

For such an argument would presuppose the existence of an emotional *nature* common to all mankind, irrespective of environment; and it would presuppose also that this emotional *nature* is unchangeable.

Such a position cannot be upheld in the face of evidence collected by anthropologists who have observed the behaviour of primitive peoples in widely different social and historic environments. Yet the unchangeable *nature* of man was taken for granted by Freud when he formulated his psycho-analytical theory. And instead of correcting the fundamentals of his theory from a reference to patterns of culture completely different from that in which all his practical psycho-analysis was done, Freud explains the behaviour of primitive people upon the basis of this unwarranted premise. Having fitted together data from anthropological research according to his own psycho-analytical theory, he uses the result to strengthen that theory.

Freud presupposes that the *nature* of mankind, wherever and whenever it manifests itself in behaviour, is the same— and, of course, this *nature* and this sameness are qualitatively and dynamically the *nature* and sameness which he has observed in our society. Malinowski, the anthropologist, falls into the same error, and poor, inoffensive Trobrianders are endowed with all the blessings and social advantages of an Oedipus complex, the attendant repressions being carefully modified to fit in with the local social organization and marriage laws.

It will be instructive for our purpose to examine in more detail the philosophical consequences of this unscientific attitude in Freud's work.

After long observation and experiment, Freud came to the conclusion that those complexes which are the root cause of neurosis have their origin in childhood experiences. Describing the progress of his clinical attitude, he says, "The patient's associations led back from the scene one was trying to elucidate to earlier experiences, and compelled the analysis which had to correct the present, to occupy itself with the past. This regression led constantly further backwards; at first it seemed regularly to bring us to puberty; later on, failures and points which still awaited explanation, beckoned the analytic work still further back into the years of childhood which had hitherto been inaccessible to any kind of exploration." [1]

The complexes, which are formed in the early years of childhood, result in the repression of emotional experiences which should be a part of the normal development of every personality. In our society, the child, throughout the period of infancy and until after school age, is almost completely dependent upon the mother for food, protection and the satisfaction of every need. The child's relationship with the mother is most important, for normally the mother is the only person who is continually with him. The mother is able to satisfy his first experiences of hunger, and she is able at the same time to afford him his first experiences of pleasure. It is to be expected, then, that the child's first pleasurable sentiments are formed in relation to his mother, and it is through

[1] *Collected Papers* : London, 1924-25, Hogarth Press.

his relationship with her that the child builds up his attitudes towards other members of the family. The child is so dependent upon his mother, and his contact with her is so continuous and so intimate, that he develops (on an infantile level) sentiments of affection and sexual love in relation to her. He wishes, further, to win and hold for himself all her affection and attention, and he is inevitably jealous of the time and attention his father claims, both in his presence by day and in secret by night.

Freud maintains that in this situation repressions are formed, involving attitudes of love, jealousy, fear, hate and aggression (again on an infantile level) in relation to the mother and father. Because the child is jealous of the father's share in his mother's affections, he secretly hates him and wishes for his removal so that the mother's love and affection will be exclusively his own. But the father's attitude towards him shows the child that really he has every reason to love his father, and that his secret attitudes of jealousy and hate are unreasonable and very wrong.[1] Thus the child develops an ambivalent attitude towards his father.[2] As a measure of protection against the guilty fears which accompany his secret longings, the attitudes of jealousy, hate and aggression are driven into the unconscious; that is, they are repressed, so that, although they are dynamically operative within the unconscious mind, they are never allowed to become conscious. In this way the conflict in the child's mind

[1] The moral code, concerning incest and the proper relation of parent and child, is made clear to the child at a very early age, and is, of course, very much responsible for the feeling of guilt and fear.

[2] This ambivalent attitude is, according to Freud, the nuclear complex of neurosis. The complex is, of course, far more complicated than is here described, and it becomes more and more complicated as future experiences attach themselves to it. For the quality of all future relationships and experiences is in some way influenced by the complex, the cause of which is forgotten and cannot be recalled except through psycho-analytical technique.

is resolved. But from this point the normal development of emotional attitudes by the child is prevented by the existence of the repressed emotional attitudes.

Now, all Freud's clinical work has been concerned with men and women who are products of our particular social pattern. And since he found sufficient evidence to justify his belief that the Oedipus complex is universal in our society, he took it for granted that the Oedipus complex is directly and inseparably related to the *nature* of man.[1] Wherever or whenever man takes up his abode he must bring with him the Oedipus complex which will inevitably determine the development of the family life, and directly or indirectly influence all his relations with his fellow-men. Such a theory is not supported by anthropological research, and the basic error, which is now apparent, distorts the significance of much of Freud's work.

In the Trobriand Islands of Melanesia Malinowski found a family life which is somewhat different from ours, and in the absence of evidence of the official Oedipus complex, he postulated its pre-existence, before the present family organization drove it deeper into the unconscious. The Trobriand family is matrilineal; the father is not the head of the family, and he has not the same economic position as the father normally has in our society. In Trobriand the head of the family is the maternal uncle, and it is through him that wealth and property are inherited. The child feels the authority of his maternal uncle to be far more significant than that of his father, for he can give or withhold economic power and possessions. On the other hand, the tribal law of incest is directed not against the mother-son relationship, but only against the sister-brother relationship.

[1] *Totem and Taboo*, by Sigmund Freud : London, 1919, Kegan Paul, Trench, Trubner & Co. Ltd.

In these circumstances, it is to be expected that the child may secretly hope for the removal of his uncle, but such an attitude can only develop when he has reached an age when economic power and independence are significant in his life—hardly during the early years of childhood. Thus the real situation in which Freud's Oedipus complex develops is completely lacking, and the evidence from tribal mythology and the dreams of the natives does not show any unconscious antagonism between the son and the father, nor any feeling of guilt from the child's wished-for relationship to his mother.

It is clear, then, that in the family organization in the Trobriand Islands the Oedipus complex proper cannot exist. The dreams and mythology of the islanders show that the strict taboo against sister-brother incest, and the authority of the uncle over the child, produce complexes in the unconscious mind; but these complexes are certainly not the same as the Oedipus complex which Freud discovered in our civilization. Nor is there any evidence that the Oedipus complex ever existed in the Trobriand mind.

The essential situation of Freud's Oedipus complex involves the mother-son-father relationships, and there is no evidence that these relationships produce any special complex in the unconscious mind of the Trobrianders. The two factors which are responsible for repressions and anxieties in the Trobriand family life are: first, a definite, strict social taboo against sister-brother incest; and, secondly, the authority, economic and social, of the uncle over the nephew.

The fundamentals of Freud's psycho-analytical theory are not supported by the facts of anthropological investigation. From the psycho-analytical point of view, as from the anthropological, the evidence for a common and unchangeable *nature* of man is not only inconclusive, but also contradictory. And since the "nuclear complex of neurosis" is taken by Freud as the basis for a great deal of his theory, it will be necessary to examine his conclusions, especially those which apply directly to Education.

Every part of his theory is based upon his knowledge of the dynamics of the conscious and unconscious mind in our society, and at this particular stage of its development. He has taken it for granted that the dynamics which characterize the growth of the mind in our society, in the present historical phase, would be active in every stage of social development, whatever its basis and background. But it has been shown, in the instance of the Oedipus complex, to which Freud attaches supreme importance, that he has made a simple error of scientific approach; that there is, in fact, no *nature* of the individual which is independent of social and historical environment. Therefore, it can be assumed that the whole structure of the mind in our society [1]—both the conscious and the unconscious mind—is not immutable; that Freud's *nature* of the unconscious, his "id," his "ego" and his "super-ego" are more or less local phenomena, dependent for their existence upon the peculiar environment of our times.

It is not too much to hope, therefore, that, with knowledge and insight, and with planning and industry, we can reconstruct society upon a different basis: that we can construct a society in which the pattern of the mind and the pattern of social behaviour will be very different from those we know today. In such a society the vicious and perverse "id," the naughty "Oedipus complex," the jealous "ego" and the Argus-eyed "super-

---

[1] And, of course, in every other society.

ego" may be filed away in the archives as "The Psychology of a Primitive Tribe."

Our new society will have nothing to do with the attitudes of jealousy, hate and aggression which, Freud implies, help to make war inevitable, and our children, bless their hearts, while enjoying all the affection of parent and society, will look upon Freud as a nasty ogre who said, "The function of Education is to inhibit, forbid and repress." [1]

The function of Education is not to inhibit, forbid and suppress. The function of Education shall be to use, guide and encourage, and the example of teacher and society as a whole, together with the active participation of the school in social life, shall lead our children from earliest years into a likeness and sympathy with the beauty of reason.

---

[1] " ' David,' said Mr. Murdstone, ' to the young this is a world for action ; not for moping and droning in.'

' As you do,' added his sister.

' Jane Murdstone, leave it to me, if you please. I say, David, to the young this is a world for action, and not for moping and droning in. It is especially so for a young boy of your disposition, which requires a great deal of correcting ; and to which no greater service can be done than to force it to conform to the ways of the working world, and to bend it and break it.'

' For stubbornness won't do here,' said his sister. ' What it wants is to be crushed. And crushed it must be. Shall be too ! ' "

David Copperfield.

CHAPTER V

PHILOSOPHY AND FASCISM

THE cleavage between philosophical thought and social practice is apparent throughout the history of western civilization. Ideals and standards of human behaviour in society, whether expressed by philosophers and artists, or preached by men of religion, have always conflicted with the practical human relationships which the economic organization of society demands.

In some phases of history the conflict has been slight, in others very sharp. During the best period of Greek culture (if we leave out the slave community upon which it was economically dependent) philosophical precept and social practice were almost reconciled. But Greek philosophy, the basis of which was abstract thinking, only succeeded in formulating ideals of thought and behaviour. Very soon these ideals were modified in the face of the changing economic life of the community. The constant modification of attitude in Greek philosophical thought after Aristotle, was an attempt to reconcile philosophy with the changing social life. But the influence of philosophy declined because its premises had not been checked against the economic basis of the social life which it intended to serve.[1]

---

[1] Compare :

" Property is necessary for the State, but property is no part of the State, though many parts of it have life ; but a city is a community of equals, for the purpose of enjoying the very best life possible."

ARISTOTLE.

and

" Everything is good ; it is not matter, a transitory thing, that rules, it must pass in order that things may be as they are, or else it would have been the cause of reason itself. It is reason that is the principle, reason is everything ; it has ordained everything from its origin and birth."

PLOTINUS.

In the later social history of Western Europe this cleavage is even more apparent. The introduction of Christianity helped, in some periods, to bridge the gap; but, as the methods of exploitation (both of labour and of the world's resources) developed under the spreading influence of the profit motive, Christian teaching changed its emphasis. First it demanded, as the price of salvation, seclusion from the contaminating influence of society; then, after the Lutheran Reformation, it stressed the importance of prayer and good works, as the foundation of the Christian life. Yet it rarely passed judgment on the conduct of trade and commerce or politics when their practice conflicted with Christian ideals of conduct.[1] It is now a widely accepted attitude that Christian teaching cannot be applied in business and political life.

From the seventeenth century onwards the economic life of the community came more and more into conflict with the spirit of the Commandments and the Beatitudes. But at no time have the leaders of religion examined the basis of our economic organization in relation to their teachings. They have examined only its consequences, which in the social life of the individual they often condemn, but about which, in the realm of politics, business and international relations, they most often maintain a discreet silence.[2] From what has been said in previous pages about the *nature* of man, the solution will be obvious: our present social pattern is responsible for the growth and consolidation of attitudes which are

[1] Christ showed great contempt for usurers and profit-makers who exploited man's necessity in order to accumulate wealth and social power.

In many countries, before the fourteenth century, usury was punishable as an anti-Christian practice.

Compare St. Matthew xxi. 12.

[2] The truth is, of course, that the organized churches are largely dependent, for their own economic resources, upon the economic devices of the community, and therefore they are unable to look upon the present economic structure of society without prejudice.

qualitatively and dynamically opposed to Christian teachings. If the *nature* of man is not a thing in itself, universal and unchangeable, and if the basic economic organization of a community has a directing influence upon the growth of that *nature*, then to ensure honesty, justice, charity and humanity in human relationships, the basic economic organization must first be examined and set right.

Plato was correct in that he recognized the supreme importance of environment in Education. He was even more to the point in demanding that this environment should reflect, *at every point*, the highest standards of conduct and the highest conceptions of order, reason and beauty. But neither the platonic method of Education by seclusion, nor the teaching of Christianity can do much to build a new society if the Educational environment is at *any* point separated from the social life of the community.

During the present world war the conflict between philosophical thought and human behaviour has become so sharp that it is no longer possible to reconcile the two. Only the doctrines of Fascism can justify the latest manifestations of man's *nature*. But Fascism is no philosophy: the true function of philosophy includes:

(1) the examination of the sum total of human knowledge at every stage of its growth:

(2) the relating of this total of human knowledge and experience to the world's resources and man's needs:

(3) the examination, criticism and reforming of the standards of human behaviour, and of the quality of social relationships which develop from (2):

(4) the formulation, and description to the minds of

men, of new points of contact with the mother earth; and the directing of man's mind towards the solution of new problems, so that the whole life and experience of mankind may be raised to new levels of culture and enjoyment.

Whereas the object and temporary achievement of Fascism has been:

(1) to suppress scientific thought and experiment, except such as can be used for the attainment of economic domination:

(2) to amass as much as possible of the world's economic wealth, so that it may be utilized to conquer access to the rest; and to utilize the sum of human knowledge and achievement primarily for this purpose:

(3) to train, encourage and command a standard of human behaviour which, by its horror, degradation, bestiality and complete lack of reason, is designed to terrify the rest of humanity into total submission:

(4) to withhold from mankind any opportunity for cultural progress, and by the ruthless application of suppression and horror at home and abroad, to stifle all criticism.

Fascism is the negation of true philosophy; it is at war with religion and philosophy; it fights to destroy sympathy, understanding, confidence, love and every attitude which binds mankind together. That is because the economic organization of the Fascist State is the direct negation of those fundamentals upon which these attitudes may grow and express themselves freely in practice. Fascism defends the exclusive domination of the economic resources of the State by a small, yet powerful group of profit-makers. It restricts freedom of competition in the economic field, either amongst wage-earners or owners of the means of production: for the former restriction soon changes to prohibition and suppression, for the latter restriction leads to jealous and suicidal monopolies.

The worst effects of Fascism are seen in the results of its Educational practice, for it fosters and encourages the growth of those vicious drives to action which Freud ascribes to the *nature* of man, but which are basically and completely the product of existence in contemporary bourgeois society. Under the domination of Fascism these drives to action develop a new quality and a new significance in behaviour which makes them most dangerous and most abhorrent.

It should be clearly understood that no malevolent devil of primordial ancestry is responsible for setting up in the German, Jap or Italian (or Russian for that matter) an inborn *nature* which must for ever separate their way of life from ours. The *nature* of the German, Jap or Italian is a product of more recent times, built admittedly upon previous history. But the qualities of cruelty, ruthlessness, blind unreasoned obedience and vile moral degradation which characterize the behaviour of Fascists, in war as in peace, are related only to the *nature* of Fascism. The *nature* of Fascism depends upon the economic order it was designed to protect.

The basis, development and consequences of Fascism were described by Soviet thinkers even before the rise of Adolf Hitler. Upon their analysis of the new social phenomena, and upon their observation of its subsequent behaviour, Soviet leaders planned to meet its certain menace. Even now, after nine months of war, the Soviet people are well on the way towards liquidating this menace to civilization; and they know only too well and too surely that the overthrow of Fascism entails the complete overthrow of the economic structure which bred and fed such a hideous abortion.

Man must remember for all time the barbaric behaviour of these monsters; how gangster-like they seized power, how they persecuted the Jews, how they broke up the trade unions and co-operative societies and reduced the workers in their lands to the position of slaves, how they interned in cruel bondage the freest hearts and most gifted intellects in their society, how they made a desert of peaceful Spain and gloated over the inhuman destruction in defenceless Abyssinia. But first and last and for all time must it be remembered that they betrayed the most sacred mission of humanity; they cut off their children from the milk of civilization, reason, and trained them to become wild beasts.

The child is defenceless against the ever-present influence of social environment; in the school he is equally defenceless in the face of blatant propaganda in teaching and in text book, and in face of a school organization and discipline which encourages and rewards achievements which show blind, unreasoned obedience, fanatical hero worship, even cruelty, meanness and hate. The Fascist system of Education has prided itself in the standard of health and physical culture which it achieves. Yet instead of being a blessing to themselves and to humanity, these millions of healthy men were destined, from the start, to become a curse—a curse which will be for ever on the lips of mankind.

The health and efficiency of the human body must be always a first consideration in Education; but the mind too needs special care; it must be developed truly and to full capacity. Better kill the body too, if you must kill the mind. Mind and body must be a real unity, and social behaviour is the first manifestation of this unity. But "a sound mind in a sound body" is a conception which depends for its materialization upon man's ability to build a sound social environment. And a sound social environment can result only when the basic economic activities of mankind are shared by all, consciously planned by all, consciously evaluated and enjoyed by all, and the products thereof shared by all. A sound mind cannot exist in a social environment where man's basic necessities, food, clothing and shelter, are the sport of a tiny minority of the community which owns the mother earth and the means of using its riches. Such a condition fosters hunger, discontent, jealousy, hate and aggression. The machinery which has been developed to keep such a system going needs the crude oil of propaganda, an ever-growing force of police and spies, and, in the last resort, the concentration camp, to inhibit and repress these attitudes.

Good food and the right kind of food is requisite for the development and maintenance of a healthy body; and so it is for the development and maintenance of a healthy mind. The greatest source of food for the mind is found in the child's practical experiences within society. Make our schools as perfect as the Garden of Eden, and set the twelve Apostles over them as teachers, yet will the Education prove unsound if the children leave this garden each night to dwell in a society such as ours.

The social life of the community, down to its smallest details, must go hand in hand with the formal and general Education of the community. If, because of our conception and belief in man's humanity to man, we dare face the colossal task of this world war, and accept, as the price of escaping Fascism, great sacrifice and much misery, then we can face with glowing anticipation the greater task of reconstructing our society upon a worthier foundation. The horrors of war must never be repeated. There are those in our society who would rather sacrifice

D

man's heritage of reason than sacrifice their wealth and power.[1] Let them beware lest they make a mockery of the millions dead, whose bodies held back the Fascist hordes so that our children might "dwell in a land of health, amid fair sights and sounds, and receive the good of everything; and beauty, the effluence of fair works, shall flow into the eye and ear, like a health-giving breeze from a purer region, and insensibly draw the soul from earliest years into likeness and sympathy with the beauty of reason."

[1] I recollect a professor of Philosophy who lectured on " The True Meaning of Democracy " in Dundee, Christmas 1940, saying : " There will come a time when many will have to decide whether to sacrifice their wealth or their principles ; I hope, but I am not quite sure which way the choice will go."

Probably he was recalling Aristotle : " When riches and virtue are placed together in the scales of a balance, the one rises and the other falls."

Compare St. Matthew xix. 22 :

" But when the young man heard that saying, he went away sorrowful : for he had great possessions."

CHAPTER VI

A NEW CONCEPTION OF EDUCATION

THE new conception of Education depends upon two fundamentals which have emerged from the foregoing analysis.

(1) No part of the mental and emotional life of the individual is independent of the historic environment in which the individual lives. Human *nature* does not include factors or qualities which are universal. To express it another way, human *nature* is not a thing in itself, unchanged and unchangeable, a thing part from the economic and social environment. The *nature* of man, in so far as it is demonstrated by his behaviour in society, depends for its emotional and intellectual qualities upon the social environment in which that *nature* developed. But the relationship between this *nature* and the social environment is not just one-sided. The *nature* of man, determined by social environment, influences, and in turn changes, the social environment. The *nature* of man and his social environment are, then, interrelated; and their continual interaction, one upon the other, results in vital and fundamental changes in each.

The state or condition of this fundamental relationship at any time in history is manifested by the behaviour of man in relation to his fellow-men—or, on a different level, in the behaviour of one social group in relation to another.

The emotional dispositions which characterize man's relations with his fellows are, then, clearly dependent upon the social environment for their essential quality. They are not innate dispositions, capable only of cursory modification by social environment with all it includes. Therefore the *nature* of man cannot be blamed for the behaviour of individuals or social groups; nor can it be made the excuse for man's inability to follow religious and philosophical precept.

How, then, can man understand and in some measure control the growth of his *nature* in relation to the social environment? The answer requires the consideration of our second fundamental.

(2) As the *nature* of mankind depends for its essential quality upon the social environment, so does the *nature* of the social environment depend, for its essential quality, upon the economic organization by which the society produces and distributes the necessities and enjoyments of life. This economic organization determines, in no uncertain way, the whole structure of the social environment. The basic and most necessary relationship of man to man is economic. If the accepted economic order, or the degree of economic development within the order, compels man to strive against man for the basic necessities of life, then attitudes of jealousy, competition, fear, hate and aggression must develop in the *nature* of man.

It used to be the accepted idea that instincts (especially the bad ones) had been built up during a long period of struggle and toil to win from Nature the food and protection necessary for survival. The evidence for such a theory of instincts in homo sapiens is no longer worthy of consideration. That attitudes and qualities, which are shown consistently in man's social behaviour, appear fixed and unchangeable in human *nature* is due, not to man's struggles in the distant past, but rather to the persistence of an economic structure of society which perpetuates the conditions of the past.

An economic structure which demands that man must

compete rather than co-operate with his neighbour in the economic life, and which permits the domination of the economic interests of one section of the community by the other section, cannot produce a unified social structure. Economic necessity and rivalry will tend to separate the members of the society; there can be no unity of purpose, no common aim, no sharing of activity, no fellowship, no social consciousness, in the fullest sense of the terms.

On the other hand, when the sum of man's knowledge and experience is capable of winning from the earth enough of the necessities and pleasures of life to satisfy the needs of all, a new economic organization can be adopted. The old basis can be scrapped and a new incentive to labour substituted. A common ownership of the earth, and of the man-discovered resources for converting the products of the earth into useful commodities, is now possible: a common purpose, a common plan, and the strongest of all fellowships—the fellowship of purpose, work and achievement—must, of necessity, follow. All these relationships bind men together, and the result must be a unified social structure with a unified social consciousness. Under such conditions, those attitudes and tendencies which we fear in humanity— hate, jealousy, fear, aggression—cease to exist, for the relationships which gave them birth and fostered their growth no longer exist.

That is not to say that mankind will become incapable of experiencing *attractive* and *repellent* attitudes; but it is clear that these attitudes will not have those essential qualities by which they are known in our society.

Man will know no fear, he will become for the first time potential master of his own destiny; no difficulty, no problem, but he will attempt its solution with confidence and pride.

Hate there will always be; hate of disease, ugliness, ignorance, and every social condition which withholds a possibility of enjoyment, happiness and social consciousness.

Aggression there will always be; the relentless fight against these objects of man's hate.

The whole social pattern and the *nature* of man, through their interrelationships with the economic organization, will form a complete unity. Their interpenetration, one with the other, will continually produce new levels of achievement and perfection on the one hand, and new levels of consciousness and anticipation on the other. Only upon this basis can man understand and control the development of his *nature*. Only upon this basis can there be unity between theory and practice, between man's consciousness and his actions.

CHAPTER VII

PURPOSE IN EDUCATION

SINCE these two fundamentals are interdependent they may be stated together as a fundamental relationship; the changing *nature* of the individual in relation to the planned economic organization which has been described. The result of this relationship must be a changed and changing pattern of society.

It will be changed because the growing consciousness of common ownership and common responsibility will generate an enthusiasm and a purpose in the activities of the social and economic life which are not present today. As the new economic and social relationships prove themselves in actual practice, the purpose behind man's labour will attain a new and fuller meaning; and so will the purpose of every activity in the life of social man be strengthened by a new significance and the consciousness of a new power.

In the present social and economic environment almost every activity is directed by selfish motives—by the desire, on the part of the individual or group, to secure economic advantage at the expense of others. The result is a complicated pattern of interrelationships (between the individuals concerned) which never knits itself into a united whole. The attitudes of selfish competition, jealousy and fear which, in some degree, accompany every activity, restricts its fulfilment both in quality and in quantity. A tremendous potential of human energy, physical and mental, is dissipated amongst petty conventions, restrictions, regulations, personal scruples and evasions which cloak the real *nature* of the individual relationships in our society. Instead of forming a united system of forces, the resultant of which is consciously planned and evaluated, the creative power of the individual directs itself towards any object which offers personal gain or satisfaction—anywhere and anyhow—and the result has significance only for the individuals immediately concerned. Under these circumstances the wealth of human intellect and experience makes but a small contribution to the common good and to the course of human progress. Man's mind and his body have become the slaves of complicated conventions, habits, customs, prejudices, restrictions and petty regulations which have developed and consolidated themselves as a part of our peculiar social and economic life.

There is no common purpose, no common consciousness of common needs. The energies of mankind are split, diverted and tangled between confused and make-believe loyalties. Instead of uniting themselves into an irresistible force, making full use of all man's experience and knowledge, to attain an object which will satisfy the needs of many, the energies of men expend themselves in isolation, protecting the needs and satisfaction of the individual or the few.

This confusion and lack of unity is, of course, reflected in the Educational life of the community. Within the school the child may willingly co-operate with others to achieve some immediate end—to produce a play, to write a magazine, to win a football match, or to make a toy—yet the end in view has no social significance for the child; indeed, it is a purpose with only half a meaning, for it is conceived and fulfilled in comparative isolation.

When there is little enthusiasm in the home there will be little within the school. By many parents the home is regarded as a refuge from work; for others the cinema and the club come to be a refuge from both home and work. Work in factory or office has no significance in the home; social problems, the needs of others and the needs of all, are in no way related to man's work—much less to his social activities in general. So within the school: the activities take place in an artificial environment because they are not related, in the consciousness of the child or the teacher, to a unified purpose in the life of the community outside school. And only when this relationship is fulfilled will it be possible to solve the problem of purpose in Education.

It will always be difficult for the child to grasp the significance of an activity which takes place in isolation, and which is not manifestly related to the practical life he knows outside school. The meaning which springs automatically from any activity for which a child shows aptitude and inclination is not in itself a complete meaning. The full meaning of single activities depends upon the meaning of the whole sum of school life together with the social life outside school. There can be no real separation between the work inside school and the experience of the child in society. The two fields of Education must be not only complementary but unified.

The social and economic environment is where the child will test out the knowledge and experience gained in school, and where that knowledge and experience will be given real significance. The whole social milieu into which the child enters must be a source of inspiration, determination and discipline.

But nowadays the child rarely becomes aware of the significance of his school activities through his contact with the social life around. And, therefore, the task of making school work meaningful and purposeful often evolves upon the school itself, that is, in the main upon the teachers.

It is no easy task. In general its urgency varies according to the immediate social milieu where the children live. In the Secondary, Technical and Selective Central Schools the higher level of intelligence of the children, their personal ambitions and interests, and the encouragement of their parents often provide a key to the problem. But in our Elementary Schools the teacher is often faced with apathy rather than enthusiasm.

In school work, as in the activities of adults, the recognition of a worthwhile purpose produces a diligency, a persistency and a self-discipline which no other incentive can give. The teachers have long been aware of the value of purpose in Education, and many methods of approach have been tried in order to stimulate or manufacture this consciousness in relation to the various school activities.

The child who has a strong ambition to qualify for a particular vocation finds his own interest and meaning in some or all of the school subjects and activities. A teacher, by his own enthusiasm and outstanding ability, often stimulates the same enthusiasm and ability in members of his classes. By using "The Play Way" a resourceful teacher can devise interesting and purposeful activities by which the children learn as they enjoy. And friendly competition within the school—often stimulated by home encouragement (and family pride!)—under the guidance of a capable teacher, may produce industry and purpose amongst seemingly apathetic children.

Then again a good teacher is always most careful with the arrangement of the subject matter of each syllabus and lesson. The facts and illustrations are arranged so that they are coherent and meaningful, for if the child can readily see meaning and purpose in the reasoned presentation of the subject material, he will be more likely to apply himself to the task of understanding it.

This principle is most successful when applied to the "Project Method of Teaching," or to some of its many adaptations. Some children are guided in the task of collecting and arranging information around a set theme or problem; others may be required to organize activities and experiments to the same end. This method has many advantages: it gives plenty of scope for initiative, originality, imagination and experimentation, yet it lends itself easily to co-operation and group work. Further, the Projects claim the interest of the children because they can visualize the problem as a whole, and because they have the satisfaction of visualizing and achieving its completion.

All these circumstances, principles and ideas—and many more—are readily used by our teachers, yet, except in rare instances, where the exceptional personality of the teacher or the outstanding ability of the class help to solve the difficulty their own way, it still remains a most urgent problem to induce this consciousness of purpose in school work.

But, why should it be a problem at all?

Why should it be necessary to manufacture interest, meaning and purpose in order to induce our children to seek and absorb knowledge and experience? All children delight in solving problems, in finding out the why and the wherefore of everything, and in exploring all the possibilities of their environment. Most of their play activity consists in this very thing. Healthy children have boundless energy and enthusiasm, and the more they use of it the better they like it.

It is not that the school subjects in themselves are without interest for children. Geography, History and Science, for example, can answer many of the problems which children invariably ask:

What is it like living in a strange country?
Why are most foreign people different from ourselves in colour, dress, habits, customs and beliefs?

How do we help them, and how can they help us?

How has our way of life been built up, our towns, homes, factories, industries, laws, customs, beliefs and institutions?

How do things work?

Who made them, when and why?

How do people come to think of inventions?

What will be the great inventions of the future?

In the language of children these are some of the problems which their reading, games and everyday experience suggest. There is, then, some incentive for the children to seek knowledge from these subjects. Yet too often they are the least successful of all school subjects. The sum total of the average child's knowledge of history is usually a mass of unrelated facts and impressions which explain nothing. Our teaching of social history produces only a slightly better result.

History has no real meaning for the child: the social and economic life of the past is not directly related, in any practical way, to the present-day experiences and aspirations of the child. At the best our history lessons satisfy the child's curiosity, but fail to satisfy the intellect. If the knowledge so gained helps the grown child to adjust himself or herself to the complicated pattern of social life—which is very doubtful—it certainly does not lead to any understanding of the *nature* of this pattern, nor does it help the adult to participate in its progressive transformation. The meaning which can be attached to history study, so long as the school is isolated from society, is less than half a meaning, for the subject is not directly and practically related to the social and economic life of the community.

And so with geography and science. To achieve its end our Educational System makes use of the child's curiosity, his love of practical activity, his spirit of wonder, admiration, emulation and his credulity, but it neglects the great essential—because it has to. Our social structure protects itself by being unknowable, and Education in general retains its self-respect by only pretending to make it knowable.

The knowledge included in these subjects, geography, history and science, is the very foundation of human progress. These branches of knowledge comprise the total of man's experience in the past, his knowledge of the world's resources, and the results of man's efforts to evaluate and utilize these resources. Essentially, history and geography must include the study of man in relation to his environment. For complete understanding of this relationship the two subjects must become one; so unified they can give perspective and significance to the modern achievements of the human mind, the practical sciences, and the social sciences—psychology and sociology.

What of the arts and crafts? Judged upon the basis of the children's enthusiasm for these subjects and the results obtained, this is, perhaps, the most successful branch of Educational activity. Children delight in these forms of self-expression, they like to display their dexterity in painting, drawing, woodwork, metalwork and every other art and craft: most of all they find satisfaction in designing and constructing things, especially models, apparatus and fitments which are useful in the home, in school, or for their own devices.

Given sympathetic guidance and adequate facilities, the children will develop great enthusiasm for these activities, and they will apply themselves to mastering the skills with a diligence which often contrasts sharply with their apathy towards other school subjects. It is the practical nature of the activities, the appeal of colour and shape, the tangible and easily demonstrable results which win the child's active co-operation. But to make the child realize the practical usefulness of these skills in the social life generally is a more difficult problem. Within the narrow circle of the school or the home it is easy; but what of the life after school? To prepare for that is the first object of Education. If it is "Education for Leisure," then the trained abilities and skills may afford pleasure in adult life provided that the right kind of leisure for exercising them exists. How rarely it does. The growing sense of insecurity, the prevailing attitude of apathy towards the daily tasks of life, the lack of true fellowship man with man, the fearful sense of isolation drive our people to other ways of occupying their leisure hours—ways which lull the senses, suspend anxieties and grant distorted dream-like satisfaction to their secret hopes and plans. The pride of craftsmanship is dying, smothered in the ruthless and impersonal market, and art is almost completely divorced from the practical life of the community. The world outside school has little time—and no encouragement—for arts and crafts for their own sake. They are enjoyed only in isolation by the few, and, more often than not, scorned by the many. Few of their achievements raise the social consciousness to a sense of unity and pride, as did the drama and folk music of Shakespeare's time, or, as now, the theatre and palaces of culture do in Soviet Russia.

Thus our children find no added meaning for their efforts in the world outside school, and they can only look upon the joy of the craft room and the pleasures of artistic expression and creation as things apart from the social life at large. The best that can be hoped for art and craft education in this society is that the children will acquire the skills and the confidence to increase the amenities of their future homes; that it may provide consolation and a measure of satisfaction to the individuals who live isolated from their fellow-citizens.

Most teachers will readily agree that the Senior School period of the child's education is the time when lack of enthusiasm and purpose becomes a most serious problem. During the years 11 to 14 the boys and girls become more and more conscious of the activities of adult life. They are conscious of its privileges and its possibilities, they are aware of their growing physical powers, and they are constantly reminded of their economic dependence upon the family. More often than not our Elementary School children are impatient to leave school so that they can share the economic burden of the family—and, by so doing, attain a state of freedom and autonomy which, they imagine, is the blissful privilege of adults.

The children, during the last years of their school life, are looking forward to the time when they will enter the social life of the community as "men and women." And it is then that they should be aware of the relationship between school activities and the world outside. For from this awareness would spring a new and vital purpose which would give a new meaning and a new enthusiasm to all the school activities. But the children can be aware of no such relationship, for none exists. The school—in so far as it is a community—is an isolated community. Its teaching, its activities, its standards of behaviour and the moral codes which it sponsors as ideals are all completely divorced from the child's practical experience of the social life as a whole.

If the economic organization in our society tears men apart and holds them apart so that, through their basic activities, they experience no feelings of fellowship, no consciousness of a common aim, nor the binding comradeship of a common achievement, then it is useless to hope that any real unity can exist between life in school and life in this community outside. The people of Bath are not conscious of any fellowship with the miners of South Wales or the fishermen of Hull; the people of Stepney and Hampstead are not aware of any common purpose in their daily life; very often, may it be said to their shame, the different grades of a single industrial organization are not united by any consciousness of a common interest. There is nowhere any common consciousness, nor any philosophy, nor any faith which can bind this society together into a purposeful and progressive unity.

Even now (May 1942) when freedom and humanity are threatened, selfish interests, jealousies and fears jeopardize our national integrity and weaken our total effort. There are many whose actions suggest that they would rather lose the war than sacrifice a prejudice which protects their economic interests. The degree of unity of purpose which the hatred of Fascism has created in the minds of our people is strained and torn by the economic structure within which they strive to achieve their purpose.

The social milieu in which our children live is a far more powerful instrument of education than are our schools. Its influence overrides all educational effort, and all that our schools can do is to provide a shelter from this influence. Within this shelter, as within the home, our children are taught all the social virtues, all the ideals of reason, order and beauty which our society cannot put into practice. In its family life the child learns to know and value affection, love, mutual loyalty and trust: in the world of business and in the social life generally the same child meets the very antitheses of these attitudes. The school fosters the social attitudes which characterize family life at its best. It is as if we deliberately seek to hide the realities of life from the child during the period of education, instead of helping the child to face these realities. In effect, the child is taught that the realities of life are unreal and wrong; that the unrealities are real and true. But long before the child leaves school his contact with the social life around teaches him what is real and what is unreal, and to reconcile the two he must adopt all the adult social attitudes, which include apathy and hypocrisy.

The only practical purpose which our teachers and parents can hold out to the children is the necessity of preparing themselves to hold their own and compete with others in the coming struggle for work and economic security.[1] And this certainly is no make-believe purpose for the children in our society. But by promising the child opposition from society instead of co-operation, by making clear to the child the possibility of insecurity instead of the certainty of security, by putting a premium on selfish competition instead of upholding the value of true comradeship, this purpose violates every standard of human behaviour and every enlightened conception of Education. It throws philosophy to the winds.

This is no true purpose for our children. Society alone can provide the answer: it must build itself anew so that it is fitted to play its part in Education, in unity with our teachers and our schools. The true purpose of Education must be inherent in the social and economic life of the people. Then will our children know their real worth. They will know that their great purpose in life is not to strive against other men for economic advantage and security; rather it is to contribute jointly, one with another, to satisfy the common economic

---

[1] To thousands of our city children whose fathers and brothers have been demoralized by long periods of unemployment and economic insecurity this is obviously a futile purpose to hold out.

E

needs.   To achieve this purpose—to participate in the common social and economic tasks—is the child's right; and herein is his right to share with all others the fruits of the common effort.   He must know that these are his rights and believe in them.

When our children know from the example of the social life they share that the community needs all their efforts, all their enthusiasm and all their inventiveness, and when they know that society will value and reward these efforts, then will our children develop all their abilities to the full; then will society be enriched beyond measure.   Then will the problem of Purpose in Education be solved.

CHAPTER VIII

THE PROBLEM OF DISCIPLINE
THE POSITION OF THE TEACHER
INDIVIDUALITY IN EDUCATION

THE PROBLEM OF DISCIPLINE

OUR Educational practice shows that it is still a generally accepted idea that the function of Education is to inhibit, forbid and suppress the *natural* anti-social *instincts* of the children. This idea, to which Freud has given expression in psychological terms, has already been discussed. It presupposes an *instinctive nature* of the individual which includes drives to action of an inherently anti-social character. These *instinctive* drives to action are anti-social because they strive to obtain self-satisfaction without regard to the appeals of reason and in spite of the consequences upon other members of the social group.

But it has been pointed out that this conception of human *nature* is the result of examining human behaviour in our specific historic environment; that, in fact, there is no such thing as a *nature* in humanity apart from historic environment. The quality of these blind and vicious impulses, which Freud calls upon Education to suppress, is due not to the universal and unchangeable *nature* of man, but to the historic social and economic environment wherein Freud carried out his observations and experiments. If the *nature* of our children did include urges to selfish, unreasoning, rebellious actions, then (cynicism not implied) it would be almost impossible to devise a social environment more suitable than our own for fostering such drives to action.

It is quite wrong to adopt the attitude that we must

gradually wear down the *natural* tendencies and desires of the children with a view to making them gradually conform to adult standards of behaviour.[1]   Such a method of obtaining discipline in our schools has been challenged repeatedly, but in practice it is still widely followed.   It could be considered a correct form of discipline only if it were agreed that the object of Education is to consolidate and perpetuate the moral codes and standards of behaviour which, in actual practice, characterize our present phase of civilization. For, if it is argued that within the school our children are trained to conform to ideals and standards of behaviour which are sponsored by religion, philosophy and well-tested tradition, then we are immediately faced with the problem of School versus Environment; and enough has been said already to show that Environment is the more potent influence in present-day Education.

The basis of this repressive form of discipline can be traced to the *nature* of the social and economic environment.   It has been demonstrated in previous sections of this essay that the economic relationships of individuals, groups and classes in our society foster attitudes of selfish competition, jealousy, fear and hate, and that the quality of these attitudes is intrinsically derived from this peculiar economic organization.   Yet if society allowed the full and free development of these very attitudes which its economic organization nourishes, it is obvious that the result would be chaos—it would very soon cease to be a society at all.

In order that our society may retain its stability, it is

---

[1] " Children must be children before being men," said Rousseau.   But that is no excuse for regarding them as little animals because their unbounded enthusiasm, energy and curiosity often lead them to behaviour which conflicts with our adult standards of conduct and self-discipline.

Children are not little animals, neither are they little men.   They belong to the species homo sapiens, certainly, and they will do honour to that name unless the adult environment makes them as unwise as itself.

necessary, therefore, for some form of discipline to hold in check the expression of these *natural* dispositions. The forms of discipline which society imposes upon its members are as varied and complex as the complicated pattern of our society suggests.

Within the school, and in society generally, there are upheld certain moral standards of behaviour derived from abstract philosophy, from long usage, or from a constantly modified legal code. These forms of restraint are variously enforced by the authority of learning and religion, tradition and convention, or more simply by an ever-increasing police force. They prove effective, however, only so long as the expanding economic organization does not impose more urgent restriction upon the economic life of the individual, group or class. But once this situation arises, these forms of discipline need reinforcing, either by other forms of restraint newly devised, or by taking upon themselves a harder, or even a harsh quality of repression, supported by more complicated and more effective police methods.

During the present century, and more especially since the Great War of 1914 to 1918, the public has become aware of a new moralizer, a new guide to thought, feeling and action—propaganda. Propaganda has become a consciously planned technique by which public opinion is influenced and moulded. It is used very effectively to serve the interests of individuals, groups and classes in our society. By appealing to the basic longings, the most pressing fears, and to the class prejudices of the individual in our society, it is used in business life to increase the sales of commodities, good, bad and indifferent, while in political life it is used to bemuse public opinion and to win mass support in such a way that "democratic" principles are served without sacrificing economic interests. Propaganda appeals to any authority to gain its end; religious tradition, social convention, the authority of a great name, or the weight of public opinion. Its most potent ally is the confused state of the public mind, which accepts contemporary conditions as inevitable and unknowable, and which by its very *nature* prefers incompetence and complacency to decisive actions which might prejudice the already precarious economic interests of the individual.

These forms of discipline, in a multitude of disguises, are an essential part of the whole fabric of social life. But the fabric has no longer a real pattern; the weft and the warp are now invisible, hidden by patches, darns, adhesive tape and sticking-plaster which cover the slits of fortune and the ravages of time. The *nature* of the individual born of the social pattern, the whole mass of customs, habits, conventions, traditions and prejudices which could exist in no other pattern of society, all help to hold the fabric together. To change the metaphor, they have become like dutiful children who give succour to a parent who has grown old, worn and decrepit through his struggles to win sustenance for them in a land of plenty.

Eventually man's reason and his necessity rebel against the incongruity of incomprehensible restrictions in a world of plenty. As man's intellect discovers new and more efficient ways of utilizing the world's resources, so does his capacity to use and enjoy these resources expand. But our economic organization, while making good use of the new achievements of man's mind to consolidate economic power in the hands of the few, imposes ever more and more restrictions upon the enjoyment of the fruits of these achievements in the social life generally. The very *nature* of our economic system demands these restrictions as the price of its stability. Herein lies the *nature* of our repressive form of discipline.

Only upon this basis is it possible to explain the gnawing conflict between Educational theory and practice in so far as it affects discipline in Education. The educationist's knowledge of the possibilities of a discipline which is inseparable from meaningful and purposeful activity is far ahead of Educational practice. In fact, it may be justly stated that this new principle (which owes much to the new science of psychology as applied to Education) has had little or no influence upon Educational practice and achievement commensurate with the obvious possibilities it holds out.

The conflict between what learning and philosophy claim as a possibility, and what teachers can and do achieve in actual school practice, will not resolve itself until the circumstances which make for a repressive form of discipline in Education are removed. It has been pointed out that the *nature* of the individual in our society and the *nature* of the restrictions and repressions which hold the society together are interdependent, and that the peculiar qualities of each are due to the basic economic organization upon which our social pattern is built. The only way to create the Educational conditions under which a repressive form of discipline is unnecessary is, therefore, to change the fundamental relationships which comprise the economic basis of our society. The usual approach to the problem—which is nothing more than an excuse for the obvious conflict between theory and practice—is to blame the *nature* of the individual. But such an approach brings us back to the futile, unscientific position of Freud.

The function of Education is not to inhibit, forbid and suppress. Any system of Education which "performs this function to admiration" is a futile system of Education. It may mould docile citizens for the future, but, at the same time, it will inhibit vast emotional and mental resources within the child's mind. The true function of Education is to develop in the children every capacity to the full, so that, as children and as future citizens, their contribution to the common store of knowledge and achievement will be a maximum contribution. This can only be assured if the child knows from his experience within society that, reciprocally, his share of the commodities and enjoyments of life will be a maximum share.

Interest, meaning, purpose and discipline are interdependent aspects of one problem in Education. Upon the solution of this problem as a whole depends the whole future of Education. The great essential in all Educational activity is consciousness of purpose. If the children are fully conscious of a worthwhile purpose which their activities can serve, then interest and meaning will be present always, and the problem of discipline will solve itself. But it will be a new kind of discipline; it will be a self-discipline which controls the children's thoughts and behaviour as they expand to reach the objects of the purposeful activity. Instead of being repressive, its function will be to control, according to the laws of reason, an ever-expanding vision of possibilities and an ever-increasing inventiveness. Instead of trying to inhibit, forbid and suppress the *natural* impulses of the child, its object will be to encourage, guide and direct the practical expression of the child's abilities to the full. All the emotional and intellectual energy which is now expended in the service of inhibitions, suppressions and restrictions will then be freed for the service of the new purpose which is at one with all social activity.

Such a form of discipline, which is inherent in the purpose of the activity, can be successful only under the conditions described in the previous section of this essay: where common ownership of the world's resources, and of the means of making these resources useful, form the economic basis of a society wherein human *nature* is transformed. Selfish competition, jealousy, hate and fear will have no part in such a society; in their place will develop pride of achievement, true fellowship and eager co-operation, and over all a unity of purpose which will be the mainspring of self-discipline.

THE POSITION OF THE TEACHER

The fundamental attitude of most teachers and educationists is that the *nature* of the individual and the *nature* of the social structure are immutable. And this attitude characterizes all educational effort within the school. Our teachers are well aware that there is a sharp conflict between what is taught in the school and what actually takes place in the social life outside school. They know that the influence of the social environment dissipates much of their effort to train in the children attitudes of co-operation, tolerance and service, just as it undermines their attempts to create a consciousness of a worthy purpose in life generally and in school work in particular.

Within the school our teachers set before the children, by precept and example, ideals of behaviour which conflict sharply with social practice. These ideals are the product of abstract philosophy, and they have not, and cannot have, full expression in the practical human relationships outside school.

But because our teachers, like the rest of society, take it for granted that the condition of the social milieu in general is beyond human control, they are inclined to support the Churches, the Press and the Welfare organizations who point to particular aspects of the social life as the cause of educational shortcomings and moral delinquency in the children. They do not see, however, that the type of entertainment provided by the cinema and cheap literature, or the home conditions of the children, or unemployment, are merely symptoms of an organic disorder which is congenital in the present social structure. Repress the symptoms in one place and they will immediately show themselves, more or less disguised perhaps, in another place.

Many teachers fully realize the effects upon Education of unemployment, slums, poverty, malnutrition and the condition of the labour market, yet few seek to find the root causes of such conditions in our society. It is significant that teachers are discouraged—by Local Education Authorities, Inspectors, Boards of Governors and vested interests in general (disguised as public opinion)—from taking any part in the political activities which seek to remove these social evils by the roots. The teacher is permitted to do what he wishes, both in actual teaching and in social activity, to consolidate the attitudes characteristic of our social behaviour, and to perpetuate the basic structure of society. But otherwise he may not take up a position of leadership, in school or in society, on questions which affect the economic organization of our society. He must use text books for history and geography which are full of outworn ideas of imperialism, class prejudice and the like, but he is considered subversive if he trains the children to examine the facts of history and geography scientifically and from first principles. He is permitted to teach the children all about the intricacies of unemployment benefit, taxation, rates, profit and loss, etc., etc., but he is not expected to help them to create a world in which unemployment does not exist, and in which taxation is in the cause of health and happiness instead of in the cause of misery, death and destruction.

The teacher, therefore, finds himself identified with the isolated school community. His teaching is based upon principles which, he knows, have no basis in actual social practice. He imparts a store of knowledge which is unrelated to any unified social purpose—because none such exists. For the teacher and for the children there is no real point of contact between their school work and the social life outside school.

From the teacher's point of view it is clear that the knowledge, precept and example which he sets before the children will have, for many of them, but little practical value in the social life of the community as a whole.

The position of the teacher, then, is most unsatisfactory. It is an artificial position from whatever angle it is considered.

(1) Since the social life outside school provides no real unified purpose by which the school activities would be given full meaning and significance, the teacher must invent or manufacture a purpose for the children. Such a purpose, however well contrived, and however well founded upon the tenets of child psychology and experience, must be unsatisfactory.

(2) The teacher knows the incomparable value of self-discipline, the discipline which is a part of truly purposeful and meaningful activity. He agrees with this principle whole-heartedly, but is powerless to apply it to the full because truly purposeful and meaningful activity is impossible in the isolated school community, and· because the *nature* of the social system demands a repressive form of discipline.

(3) He is not permitted to do any more than try to

adjust the children to the difficulties of our social environment. Any form of approach to the problem which includes an impartial analysis of the present economic organization, present-day conventions, accepted traditions, customs and prejudices is taboo inside school or outside school.

(4) The teacher himself cannot be fully conscious of his tremendous responsibilities to society any more than society as a whole is conscious of its responsibilities to the children. Education must be a part, perhaps the most important part, of a unified social purpose, whose basis is common ownership and common interest, and whose object is the common good. But in our society the teacher must work alone in the isolated school communities, training skills which society will misuse or neglect to use at all, spreading knowledge which in society will be distorted, tangled and misplaced, and teaching moral standards of behaviour which cannot be practised in the social life we know.

What, then, is the real position of the teacher in society?

It has been made clear that the study and activity which goes on within the school constitutes only a part of the child's Education. The social milieu in which the child lives plays a most important part in determining the quality of the future citizen. But the school and the social environment must not be separate and conflicting spheres of Education; they must become a unified sphere of activity and influence wherein the child can gain knowledge and experience.

The position of the teacher, then, is most important.

He is the link between the Education of the school and the Education of the environment. It is not enough, therefore, for the teacher to have the ability to impart knowledge to children and to be able to guide and encourage their activities. His job is to look after the whole Educational life of the child. He must see that the activities of the school are given a practical significance for the children through their contact with the wider social life outside school. Conversely, he must arrange and present knowledge and organize activities within the school in such a way that the whole relates directly and practically to the social life of the community. The teacher must be ready at all times to guide and encourage the child's understanding of the social purpose, and the quality of human relationships, as they develop under the impetus of this great purpose.

To do all this the teacher himself must be a good citizen—in the fullest sense of the term. He must be an active member of society, fully conscious of the great social purpose, for the realization of which the Education of the children is all important. His knowledge and social consciousness must make him a leader and an organizer in society. He must be fully conscious of the needs, the plans and the aspirations of the people, ever ready to interpret and explain them to child and adult citizens alike. By serving the immediate aims in the social and economic life of the community he can more readily unite school activity to the wider purpose of social progress.

The teacher must be an example to the children by reason of his own social activity. He must participate in the building of the future which is to provide for all ever-increasing sources of enlightenment and enjoyment. It is necessary, first of all, for all teachers to understand their own position as citizens, for, unless they are fully conscious of their own relationship to their fellow-men and to society as a whole, they have no right to muddle the children's minds with impracticable ideas of their relationship with society, present and future.

This is a very high standard of social service to demand from our teachers. It demands no more than they are capable of giving, and no more than they will be glad to give. In the new society the teachers will be rewarded by society according to their responsibilities. But their greatest reward will be in the manifest contribution to social progress and human happiness which their efforts produce.

INDIVIDUALITY IN EDUCATION

"Every human being is entitled to as much of the great heritage of learning as he or she can absorb. He is entitled to develop his own powers, spiritual, mental, moral, physical and aesthetic, to the full extent of their possibilities."—Dr. F. H. SPENCER (*Education for the People*).

"Education of the whole man."—L. P. JACKS.

During the last thirty years of Education the emphasis has been upon the individual rather than upon the subject matter of the curriculum. The child's interests, capacities and abilities are taken as the starting-point from which all school activities are developed. Professor P. Nunn, quoting Dr. Norwood, writes,[1] "We must stress individuality in Education, individuality of pupil, of teacher, of school, for indeed it is the key position of all. If this position is lost all is lost."

The gradual reduction of the size of classes in our Elementary and Secondary Schools has made it possible for the teachers to know the children well; they have been able to understand something of the individuality

[1] *Education, its Data and First Principles* : London, 1930, Arnold.

of each child, of his peculiar problems, his interests and ambitions. They have been able to give attention to the health problems of each child, and to take into account the peculiar handicaps and advantages of the home and the immediate social environment.

This new outlook in Education, which owes much to the insight and guidance of Educational psychologists, is of tremendous importance. Certainly, nothing of this outlook, and nothing of the knowledge and experience which it has contributed to the theory and practice of Education, must ever be lost. But much more can and will be done to educate the whole man when the social environment is such that every person can develop his individuality therein to the full. The individual needs not only the facilities for self-expression, and the sympathetic guidance of teachers; it needs also the consciousness of a worthy and redeemable purpose, so that its every effort is meaningful and complete. And it is necessary, therefore, to ensure that every contribution that the individual can make to the variegated whole of human happiness will be encouraged and used by society to the full.

The individual cannot develop all his powers to the full in an isolated school community wherein the teaching and activities are not nourished with meaning and purpose from the social life outside school. Science, History, Geography, Philosophy and the Arts and Crafts are of little use in themselves. Given the facilities for their exercise, they will provide a chance of survival, and maybe a little comfort, for the lonely individual wrecked upon a desert island. But the meaning of all learning and experience is enriched beyond comparison, and their application invigorated and ennobled beyond measure, when man is conscious that this learning and experience binds him in ever richer fellowship with his fellow-men.

It must always be recognized that the individual is a part of the social whole, and that the peculiar quality of this social whole permeates every feeling, thought and action of which the individual is capable. The peculiar quality of our present social whole is too complex to be described in one word. From the foregoing analysis it is clear, however, that its ingredients include something of insecurity, anxiety, selfishness, jealousy, fear and antagonism. However well masticated and metabolized are these basic attitudes by that great organism, the social whole, their dynamic influence must permeate to the nature of the whole man. The whole man and the social whole are interdependent. No individual can completely transcend the influence of the social whole. It follows, therefore, from the nature of our social whole, that in our society the individuality of the child cannot be developed to the full extent of its capacity.

Yet, given a society whose basic economic relationships generate a dynamic system which is opposite to that which our economic life produces—a society wherein security, self-confidence, co-operation and fellowship are the foundations of human relationships—then will the individual grow to full stature. The whole man will enrich the social whole; the social whole will stimulate in the whole man ever greater and more varied efforts towards self-expression. The interdependence of man and society will produce a new and greater social whole, and give fuller and richer expression to the individuality of every citizen.

It is of fundamental importance in Education to stress the individuality of the child. But, whatever efforts are made within our schools, however lavish our equipment and however enlightened our educationists and teachers, the child's daily contact with our social whole will cramp and distort this individuality, instead of stimulating it to new and ever greater efforts towards self-expression.

The new society which we build must be such that the child is entitled and enabled to develop all his powers, spiritual, mental, moral, physical and aesthetic, to the full extent of their possibilities.

CHAPTER IX

TOWARDS THE FUTURE

IN order that we may be able to use fully all the possibilities of Education in the future it must be recognized, in practice as well as in theory, that the individual has two fundamental rights. First, every individual must know that it is his or her right to participate, to the full extent of his or her abilities, in the daily tasks of organization and production which are the basis of our social life. Secondly, if it is the right and duty of every individual to participate, to the full extent of his or her abilities, in the social tasks, it follows that it is also the right of every individual to participate fully in the common achievements.

Our factories, systems of transport and distribution, and every institution which contributes to the common good, must belong to all the people; theirs to organize, theirs to serve and theirs to enjoy. Only when the individual is conscious of his rights and powers, through his practical experiences and achievements, will he become conscious of an unselfish purpose directing his efforts. Then will he use all his abilities and all his powers to the full, for it will be clear that the greater his contribution to the common effort, the greater will be the common achievement and the greater the common good.

These are the two fundamental rights of man. They are the practical basis of a true democracy. And they are the starting-points of an era of social progress and security which will see the transformation of human nature, and a golden age of human happiness and achievement. Once these rights become the basis of our economic life, there will develop an entirely new system of individual relationships in the social life. Economic insecurity, fear, jealousy and greed inhibit and distort the economic effort as a whole, just as they falsify all human relationships. They result in only half-hearted co-operation, half-hearted purpose and half-hearted fellowship. But upon the basis of common ownership and common responsibility, economic security and pride will breed full-hearted co-operation, full-hearted fellowship and the full enjoyment of the achievements thereof. Our people will go forward into the future with long confident strides, pausing only to plan and to enjoy.

Then will our children be surrounded by the beauty of reason. Their work within the schools will be done with the same consciousness of purpose and the same pride of achievement which will characterize the social life as a whole. Indeed, the activities of the school will become a part of the great unified social purpose. The children will know that the world, its institutions and all the achievements of man's mind are theirs; theirs to enjoy and theirs to transform to ever higher and more useful standards of attainment.

The basis of such a society has much in common with the new civilization that our Russian Allies planned and built out of the ruins of the last world war. The fine texture of the civilization which they have so far achieved is now apparent to us and to all the world. Yet it must be clear, from the foregoing analysis of patterns of society, that no other people can build a pattern which is just like that of the Soviet society. The nature of their society depends very much upon their history, their geographical environment, their economic resources, and upon the heritage of economic and cultural achievement with which they started in 1917. It must be clear too that the growth of their new society has been influenced, in every detail, by the peculiar relationships which have existed between the Soviet lands and ideas and the rest of the world during these twenty-four years.

In every country, including our own, the pattern of society which emerges from the war will be determined by a similar group of factors. In Britain the heritage from the past must be used to the full in moulding the future. Our future society must retain and develop its own individuality, just as all other nations must retain and develop theirs.

But, just as in our new society each person will retain his own individuality while participating and co-operating fully in the social and economic life, so must it be in the world at large. Upon the basis of maximum participation in the common tasks and maximum participation in the results, each society will retain its own individuality, while co-operating fully in the economic whole of the world. As each person, through his individuality and co-operation, contributes to the sum of economic and cultural achievement in each society, so will each society, retaining its individual characteristics, contribute to the cultural and economic achievement of the world. It will be a world at peace.

These are not vague generalizations, unrelated to possibility. They have, as their basis, concrete and possible human relationships. We have reached a stage in our history when it is most dangerous to trifle with fundamentals. A half-hearted, tentative experiment which touches only a part of our economic and social life is of no use. Our civilization will totter and fall unless it is imbued with a new purpose and a new vitality throughout.

This purpose must be based upon a sincere and

objective analysis of possibilities, and our action must be scientifically planned and carried out upon the basis of this analysis.

In this essay the attempt has been made to find a new basis upon which our future society can be built. It is to be a society in which our children can grasp and use the great heritage of learning and achievement which is already ours. It remains now to consider what immediate action must be taken to assure this future, and to set Education in an environment where it can develop all the powers of the children to the full extent of their possibilities.

It is of first importance for the whole nation to know the nature of the future it is fighting for. This definition of peace aims must be in clear and precise terms. It must include an assurance of the rights of the individual as well as a statement of the responsibilities of the individual. It is of no use for our leaders to describe the future in vague, general terms. The building of this future must become, here and now, a part of the war effort. If we are to construct a new society wherein selfishness, jealousy, insecurity, fear and greed will no longer dominate the lives of men and women, then, even now, we must seek to remove the conditions which breed such attitudes. It has become clear that these attitudes hamper the war effort; it is equally clear that their opposites, security, co-operation, fellowship, self-sacrifice and confidence, can give tremendous impetus to the war effort. Men cling selfishly to the privileges, securities and prejudices of the present because they have no confidence in the future. Give the people practical assurances of the future and they will make far greater efforts and sacrifices to end the war and secure that future.

We must find leadership which will eliminate profit-making, selfishness and greed in every form. The great productive resources of the country must be taken out of the control of individuals and placed fully in the service of our great purpose. The workpeople of our factories must be encouraged to participate in the organization of production; they must be given practical demonstration of their fundamental rights and powers.

The war and the necessities of the future provide every reason why all the services connected with the education of our children should be more efficient than ever. The many difficulties which have resulted from the war situation must not be made the excuse for neglecting Education.

For more than three years now our schools have been very much disorganized, and, in the cities especially, the teachers who have remained are working against tremendous odds. There was no plan worked out in advance to meet the problems of Education under war conditions, and there has been no attempt to solve the difficulties as a whole during the war. Since the summer of 1938 the Local Education Authorities and the teachers have been struggling against a prolonged muddle which has involved Air Raid Precautions, Evacuation, the closing and re-opening of schools, part-time, half-time and full-time attendance, the sudden loss of staff to the Forces, the running of priority and non-priority evacuation schemes in the same city, lack of equipment, etc., etc. There was no centralized and co-ordinated policy on any of these problems. Muddle and confusion was passed on casually and thoughtlessly from Whitehall to Local Authorities and the teachers. For example, in some cities, weeks and even months passed in considering and experimenting with schemes for evacuation, because the

Government directives were vague or conflicting, or because they did not take into account local conditions, or because the maze of voluntary service and co-operation could not be sorted out against the background of uncertainty which prevailed. Local Authorities were uncertain of their powers, parents were uncertain of the intentions of the Government and the Local Authorities, and the teachers were uncertain about everything—except the effects of prolonged disorganization upon the work of the schools.

It is no wonder that there developed an attitude of hopelessness in relation to Educational achievement during the war. This attitude—that we must keep things going until the end of the war, when we shall be able to start again—is a negative, useless and hopeless attitude. It is an admission by society that it has lost its grip on the whole situation; it shows a negative attitude towards the future.

In the bombed cities especially, the teachers are doing a magnificent job of work, as wardens, fire-fighters, members of the Home Guard and organizers of emergency services. But within the schools their efforts have been frustrated by circumstances which are largely beyond their control. The cause of this frustration is to be found not only in the disorganization and muddle which has accumulated during the past five years. These are but symptoms of the real cause of this phase of inertia in Education. The real reason is that neither teachers nor children can see any future towards which their Educational effort can be directed. In Education, as in the war effort of the nation as a whole, this lack of a positive purpose, and of the consciousness of a worth while and attainable object, produces merely a day-to-day effort, a state of stagnation and inertia.

The immediate necessity in Education is for its efforts

to be given a place in the building of the future. Education must become a part of a great social plan, formulated and adopted now. Our children must know that the future is theirs; and, more important, they must know what kind of a future it is going to be. It must be the duty of the teachers to re-interpret and re-direct every school subject and every school activity towards the attainment of this future. Then every effort in Education will become a part of the great national effort to remove the menace of Fascism quickly, so that the possibilities of the future may become realities.

Amongst those Ministers whose task it will be to direct and co-ordinate our plans for the future, the Minister of Education must be given an important position. It is not necessary to emphasize that he must be selected for this position, not because of his inability to retain any other important post in the Government, but because of his knowledge of conditions, possibilities and needs in Education.

In planning and rebuilding our cities very careful attention must be given to the possibilities and needs of Education in the future. The new school buildings must be designed for smaller classes, yet they must include accommodation for communal activities; they must include rooms for recreation and hobbies. The larger school units will need accommodation for a medical staff and a school psychologist.

But society must give more than this to its children. Each city, or each city district, must provide something like the Soviet Palaces of Culture for the children. All we give at present is a corner of the public park or library, or some small, ill-equipped corner of a school which we call a Play Centre. The Children's Centres and Youth Centres of the future must be designed, not to keep the children off the streets, but to give them full opportunity and facilities for occupying their leisure time profitably and according to their individual interests and talents. They must belong to the children, and satisfy their every need for self-expression, curiosity and experimentation. Here our children will practise the art of self-government; here the children from many schools will meet to criticize and plan, and to determine their contribution to the social whole. From their schools and centres, and later from the youth organizations to which they will graduate, our children will make great contributions to the social plan. With eagerness and with tremendous energy, with minds unfettered by the past, they will grasp and use all the possibilities which the future can offer them. Their enthusiasm and their efforts will be an inspiration to the rest of society.

The facilities for Educational advance must be limited only by the possibilities of Educational achievement. This principle must apply no less in the school life and social life of the individual than in the Educational policy as a whole. From the Nursery Schools to the Universities and Technical Colleges, Education must be free. The children of the future must never be allowed to feel the restlessness which comes from economic insecurity and economic dependence upon a struggling family.

All these conditions can become realities only in a society which is unified at its basis and in its purpose. Education can be successful in preparing the children to make a maximum contribution to the variegated whole of human happiness only when human happiness is the unified aim of every social activity. The basis of such a society is economic security and social fellowship.

The possibilities of Education are limitless; as limitless as the resources of our world and the resources of the human mind. We must prepare a future wherein we can discover and use these possibilities to the full.

CONCLUSION

AFTER the war we shall have a patched-up system of Education only if we accept a patched-up social structure. And a patched-up social structure will be the unstable and unprofitable result only of a patched-up peace.

This can never be.

A new society will be born, either of reason in peace, or of reason snatched out of the turmoil of strife. Let it be born in peace, and let us start now to plan for it and to prepare for it; ante-natal care will save the mother no less than the child.

Let our new society be one in which all men share access to the resources of the world and to the resources of the human mind. Land which produces food to satisfy the needs of all must be the property of all. Machines and factories, wherein men work to change raw materials into usable commodities, must be the property of all those who work and of all those who need the commodities. The knowledge which our scientists gain by observation, experiment and thought must be applied in the economic and social life of the community for the common good. The beauty and enlightenment which our artists create must be accessible to all, understood by all and applauded by all.

We cannot dismiss these generalizations as Ideals. Attitudes of criticism and scorn in relation to these problems are born of the *nature* of our present environment. A completely unprejudiced attitude is impossible for members of the contemporary social order; but determination, a love of humanity, and, above all, reason and beauty can help to unravel our trammelled minds.

We must build a new social system which will foster attitudes that bind men together, not tear them apart. The practical human relationships must not be dependent upon an economic system which breeds jealousy, discontent, hate and fear. They must be a part of an economic system which demands common effort, and which gains its motive power and irresistible strength from a common purpose. Under such an economic system, the basis of which has been defined, loyalty, self-sacrifice, confidence and comradeship develop a new quality. And as these new social attitudes develop, their meaning and practical significance will change completely.

Examine the quality and meaning of each attitude in our present social life and we find that it is the necessities of the economic organization which modify and restrict their significance. Loyalty to one's fellow-men for us means loyalty to some fellow-men. Self-sacrifice in our pattern of society too often means only economic sacrifice. Confidence is too much allied to sentiment, prejudice and self-interest. Comradeship stops short and pauses when economic interests are at stake.

But new attitudes (which we may still call by the same name) will develop quickly within an economic environment which needs their fulfilment. And as the new society takes form, experience and community of labour, driven onwards to great achievements by community of purpose will bind society together as never before. The broad horizon of achievement will be for ever bright, for no false restrictions will cloud man's view of its infinite possibilities. Work, purpose, enjoyment, leisure, culture, art and science will attain a meaning, through their social significance, which members of our society cannot now easily understand.

The transition to such a social system will be no easy

change.   Blind faith, blind hero worship, vague senti-
mental hope are useless weapons with which to forge
the links.   Such attitudes would lead only to confusion
and reaction as in Nazi Germany.   There must be no
hesitancy, no "wait and see," no random turning of old
mossy stones, no vague promises, such as, "We shall
win through, we don't quite know how, but we shall
win."   To hope and pray for the realization of this social
life is of itself a negative contribution, as useless as it was
to hope and pray for peace while Hitler forged the tools
for war.

Even as we must be prepared to make great efforts
and great sacrifices to win the war, so must we be prepared
to make even greater sacrifices and greater efforts to win
the Peace.   It must be a Peace wherein our children
"dwell in a land of health, amid fair sights and sounds,
and receive the good of everything; and beauty, the
effluence of fair works, shall flow into the eye and ear,
like a health-giving breeze from a purer region, and
insensibly draw the soul from earliest years into likeness
and sympathy with the beauty of reason."

APPENDIX I

"THE relations existing between scientific writers and their readers are governed by rules agreed upon in advance. So far as we are concerned, there is no problem of scientific literature; and I shall therefore make no further reference to the subject. For the purposes of this analysis, non-scientific writing may be divided into three main classes. In the first we place that vast corpus of literature which is not intended to have any positive effect upon the reader—all that doughy, woolly, anodyne writing that exists merely to fill a gap of leisure, to kill time and prevent thought, to deaden and diffuse emotion. To a considerable extent reading has become, for almost all of us, an addiction, like cigarette smoking. We read, most of the time, not because we wish to instruct ourselves, not because we long to have our feelings touched and our imagination fired, but because reading is one of our bad habits, because we suffer when we have time to spare and no printed matter with which to plug the void. Deprived of their newspaper or a novel, reading-addicts will fall back on cookery books, on the literature that is wrapped round bottles and patent medicines, on those instructions for keeping the contents crisp which are printed on the outside of boxes of breakfast cereals. On anything. Of this kind of literature—the literature that exists merely because the second nature of habituated readers abhors a vacuum—it is unnecessary to say more than that there is a great deal of it and that it effectively performs its function.

" In the second class I put the two main types of propaganda literature—that which aims at modifying the religious and ethical opinions and the personal behaviour of its readers, and that which aims at modifying the social, political and economic opinions and behaviour.

" For the sake of convenience, and because it must be given a name, we call the third class imaginative literature. Such literature does not set out to be specifically propagandist, but may none the less profoundly affect its readers' habits of thought, feeling and action."

ALDOUS HUXLEY.[1]

[1] *Writers and Readers* : from *Stories, Essays and Poems*. London, Everyman's Library : Dent.

APPENDIX II

"THERE was great rejoicing in the village when it was learned that Natkusiak was going seal hunting, and all the men were anxious to go with him, partly to secure their legal share of the booty, and partly to see the hunting with a rifle. Only three of those in the village had been with us the previous summer, and they were the only ones who had seen an animal killed with a bullet.

"As a matter of local law there were two or three hunters who would not have needed to go along in order to get a share of the game, for in the division of the spoils only one piece of the seal goes to each household, irrespective of how many hunters representing it are present. The rule is that when a bearded seal is killed, the man who does the killing takes his stand on a conspicuous place near the dead animal and makes signals, usually by swinging out his arms at right angles. All those hunters near enough so they can see the sign come running up. Then the animal is divided into as many segments as there are families represented by the hunters present, and when the cutting up has been done, the most influential person present has the first choice, which means that he takes the biggest and best piece, while the hunter himself, irrespective of his standing in the community, takes the last and therefore the poorest piece, but he has the honour, which is no small thing among them, for not only is the deed considered one of prowess, but the man who provides so much food for the community thereby becomes a public benefactor, and gets a valued reward in the consciousness of increased public esteem." V. STEFANSSON, *My Life with the Eskimo*.

For Product Safety Concerns and Information please contact our EU
representative GPSR@taylorandfrancis.com
Taylor & Francis Verlag GmbH, Kaufingerstraße 24, 80331 München, Germany

www.ingramcontent.com/pod-product-compliance
Lightning Source LLC
Chambersburg PA
CBHW050539270326
41926CB00015B/3303

9 781138 007512